Florida Suncoast Housing Trends Quarterly Guide

First Quarter 2019

E.G. Ovitz SRA

Viridian Key Corp
Real Estate Appraisers
Englewood, FL 34224

Cover Photo: Fisherman's Village Marina, Punta Gorda, FL

Contents

Welcome to Florida's Suncoast

My friend Rod grew up in Sarasota. He tells a story that it snowed one winter day when he was a boy. Rod's been around like I have, so that was a long time ago. He says the kids had great fun scrapping up the snowflakes that hit the ground and with persistence they could make a snowball. According to one South Florida newspaper, a trace of snow fell from the skies on January 19, 1977 in Fort Lauderdale, on the east coast. I'm sure it snowed other times as well, but those are the two times that I can report. Historic average temperatures on Florida's Suncoast in December, January, and February range from the lower fifties to the middle seventies.

Yes, every now and then we get a freeze. So, keep one winter coat when you move down here, unless you need to make a fashion statement. If you ever experience a cold day, you may just see those fancy winter coats come out. I remember a couple of those days. The cold weather gets national publicity and the orange growers have to scramble to protect their trees with an icy spray of water. It seems that ice acts as an insulator and keeps the trees close to thirty-two degrees and helps prevents them from being killed. That didn't happen in the late 1800's when Englewood was founded. The earliest settlers were real estate promoters and visualized lemon orchards as a ready-made business venture to attract buyers to the area. Unfortunately, a freeze killed the lemon trees. The name Lemon Bay comes from that early venture.

With day time temperatures averaging in the middle seventies, we get lots of winter time visitors. The roads get crowded, the restaurants fill, and there is a crowd at just about any activity you find. We call it "Season."

According to Wikipedia the term Suncoast was coined in 1952 by St. Petersburg, Florida, Mayor Samuel G. Johnson. No offense is intended towards our friends in the Tampa Bay area, or for that matter our friends in Southwest Florida down in Ft Meyers and Naples. We all share the beautiful sunny west coast of Florida on the Gulf of Mexico. The information in our guide includes those communities between Tampa Bay and those surrounding Charlotte Harbor. They include Charlotte, Manatee and Sarasota Counties. **The purpose of our guide is to provide you with quarterly residential real estate trends; along with general information useful to buyers and sellers in our markets.**

Best regards,

Ernie

E.G. Ovitz SRA
Cert Res RD4302
Viridian Key Corp
Real Estate Appraisers
Englewood, Florida 34224

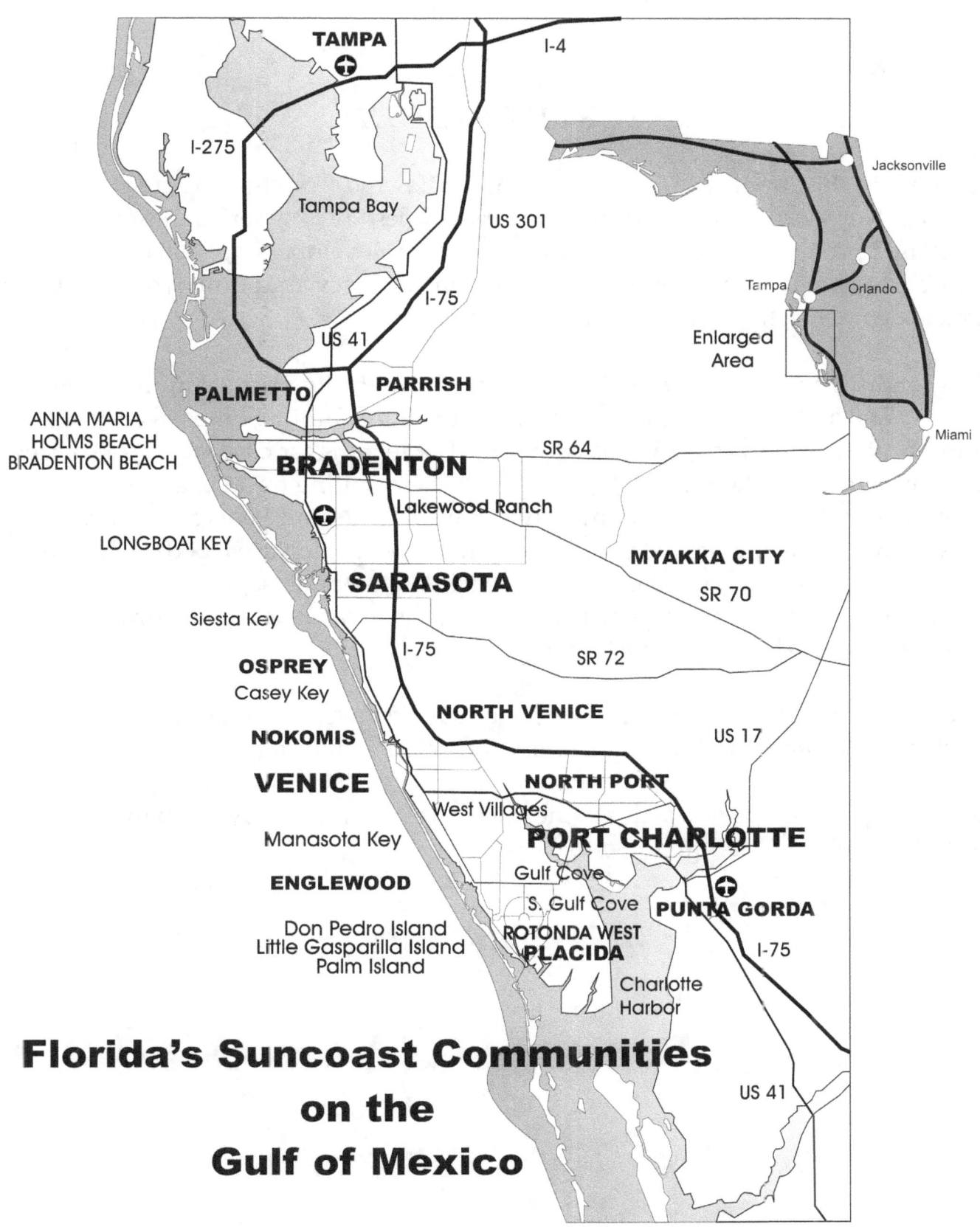

Florida's Suncoast Communities on the Gulf of Mexico

2
SURVEY RESULTS

The data in this report is derived from MFR MLS and from the appraisal files of Viridian Key Corp. The data does not include sales "By Owner" and those auctioned properties and direct sales by Builder/Developers not listed in MLS. MLS systems rely upon member participation, accuracy, and timely reporting. The data is deemed reliable, but is not guaranteed.

This report includes segmented trend charts for each city or community in our survey. The analysis divides the total sales for single family homes in each community into halves, quarters, eights, and sixteenths for each quarter reported (current quarter and going back two years.) The resulting trend charts provide a graphic illustration of each community's market tends and gives a statistical breakdown of the median (statistical middle value) heated area, bedroom, and bathroom count characteristics for the sales in each market segment. Given the disclaimer that these are sales statistics (past performance) and not current listings (available properties,) in plane language:

- You can see if the market is going up, going sideways, or going down.
- You can see generally how big a house the dollar will bring.

On the opposite page you will see the survey results ranked by Median Sale Price and Median Price per Square Foot.

Community Affordability by Median Sale Price Q1 2019

City/Community ...... Median:	$ Price	Bed	Bath	Sq Ft Heated	$/Sq Ft
Port Charlotte	190000	3	2	1578	120.41
North Port	206900	3	2	1592	129.96
Englewood	230000	3	2	1636	140.59
Palmetto	254099	3	2	1847	137.57
Punta Gorda	267750	3	2	1894	141.37
Gulf Cove & South Gulf Cove	270000	3	2	1841	146.66
Rotonda West	270000	3	2	1892	142.71
Bradenton	299900	3	2	1887	158.93
Venice	299900	3	2	1816	165.14
Parrish	299950	3	2	2164	138.61
Sarasota	318000	3	2	1830	173.77
West Villages	355496	3	2	2000	177.75
Nokomis, Osprey, North Venice	413000	3	2	2100	196.67
Lakewood Ranch	510000	3	3	2488	204.98

Community Affordability by $ per Sq. Ft. Q1 2019

City/Community ...... Median:	$ Price	Bed	Bath	Sq Ft Heated	$/Sq Ft
Port Charlotte	190000	3	2	1578	120.41
North Port	206900	3	2	1592	129.96
Palmetto	254099	3	2	1847	137.57
Parrish	299950	3	2	2164	138.61
Englewood	230000	3	2	1636	140.59
Punta Gorda	267750	3	2	1894	141.37
Rotonda West	270000	3	2	1892	142.71
Gulf Cove & South Gulf Cove	270000	3	2	1841	146.66
Bradenton	299900	3	2	1887	158.93
Venice	299900	3	2	1816	165.14
Sarasota	318000	3	2	1830	173.77
West Villages	355496	3	2	2000	177.75
Nokomis, Osprey, North Venice	413000	3	2	2100	196.67
Lakewood Ranch	510000	3	3	2488	204.98

3
FACTORS INFLUENCING PRICE

In common usage the words price, value, and cost are often used interchangeably. Real estate professionals, appraisers in particular observe the distinctions the different words have: (1) Price is a specific fact concerning one transaction; the monetary exchange made. (2) Value is an opinion of monetary worth based upon a defined standard. (3) Cost is the sum of expenditures made for land and improvements, or for a specific improved element of the property. Improvements tend to depreciate over time due to typical aging, wear and tear; and/or changing use, fashion, and functionality. Improvements also age at different rates; shorter lived improvements include: appliances, water heaters, carpets, air conditioners, etc. A longer lived improvement is roofing, while the longest lived elements would be structural. As improvements age, owner maintenance, updates, and renovations can have a significant impact on the price a specific property can command.

Buyers and Sellers look at price from opposite ends. It's no secret that buyers want a "good deal" and sellers want "top dollar." The more realistic both parties are, the more likely they will achieve an outcome satisfactory to both. The following elements are common factors that influence price in the Suncoast residential housing market:

- **Market Conditions:** rising, falling, or stable
- **Financing:** while typically available for most properties some unique properties or transactions may need special financing, require limited financing choices, or a cash sale.
- **Location:** favorable such as beach or boating access; unfavorable such as proximity to busy roads, powerlines, airports, commercial or industrial centers, etc.
- **Site or Lot Area**
- **View:** favorable such as water or wooded views; unfavorable such as views of powerlines, busy roads, commercial centers, etc.
- **Design or Style**
- **Quality of Construction**
- **Age**
- **Condition**
- **Bedroom & Bathroom Count**
- **Conditioned Living Area (Sq. Ft.)**
- **Garage/Carport and/or Vehicle Parking/Storage**
- **Porches and Patios**
- **Special amenities:** such as a private swimming pool, outbuildings, guest houses, etc.
- **Community features and amenities:** such as deed restrictions, community pools, gates, clubhouses, etc.

The relationship between the various elements noted above is often complex. For example: a lot's price will reflect the land's general location within a city, a neighborhood, neighborhood amenities, and then the property's specific location with respect to view, access to the water, or an adverse element such as powerlines. Other factors include: lot size, orientation, utility, and shape; community improvements such as: streets, curbs, sidewalks, water, sewer, gas, and communication services.

Your Real Estate Professionals: Brokers & Agents, Builders, Lenders, Appraisers, and Home Inspectors are there to assist you with the complexities of buying and selling a home. Each property is unique and may include elements and/or factors in addition to the common elements listed above.

Case Study, the Suncoast market's popular 3-bedroom, 2-bath, 2000 Sq. Ft. +- pool home:

The table below shows the first quarter 2019 results below. Please note the price variances indicated not only include the pool element, but all other factors as well. For the low sale the variance may include significant age and condition differences, the high sale variance appears to contain other significant elements such as location, view, and quality features. From my files, new pool costs over the past three years can vary from $25,000 to $100,000 or more depending upon pool size, material quality, and design features.

Q1 2019

Single Family Homes (1900 to 2100 Sq. Ft.) with and without Inground Swimming Pools

County	No. Sold	Pool	Bed*	Bath*	Sq Ft *	Low Sale	High Sale	Median Sale*
Charlotte	44	no	3	2	2004	$ 148,000	$ 700,000	$ 243,433
Charlotte	93	yes	3	2	2022	$ 174,502	$ 1,000,000	$ 310,000
Variance						$ 26,502	$ 300,000	$ 66,567
Manatee	94	no	3	2	2001	$ 145,000	$ 735,000	$ 293,250
Manatee	58	yes	3	2	2014	$ 159,000	$ 1,350,000	$ 334,500
Variance						$ 14,000	$ 615,000	$ 41,250
Sarasota	120	no	3	2	1996	$ 145,000	$ 940,000	$ 330,748
Sarasota	81	yes	3	2	2020	$ 200,000	$ 1,175,000	$ 350,000
Variance						$ 55,000	$ 235,000	$ 19,252

* Note, the Bedroom, Bath, Sq. Ft. Living Area reported is based upon median sale data.

4
FLORIDA HOMES & LIVING

Florida's humid climate and tropical weather exert a strong influence on Florida home styles and construction. A wide variety of home styles can be found including most traditional designs. However, for single family homes, the predominate Florida style is a one story design, concrete block construction, with a hip roof. Buyers can also find a variety of Florida vernacular styles such as Cracker, Key West, and Mediterranean designs. We are a *"sand"* state and concrete block is our most common local material. Wood frame construction is less common and requires extra maintenance and preservation work. Hip roofs are more wind resistant. Air conditioning is a necessity for summer living. Many Florida neighborhoods have deed restrictions and Home Owners Associations (HOA's.) If you are not familiar with HOA's, you owe it to yourself to investigate the cost, rules, and regulations that apply in any neighborhood you are considering buying in.

If you are new to our area there are some general tips that you might find helpful:

1. **Storage is at a premium**. Coastal homes are built on a slab foundation. They do not have basements. (Yes, elevated homes can be said to have a basement or ground level storage. They are a special exception.) The typical home does not have usable attic storage, as typical attics reaches temperatures of well over one hundred degrees during our long summer. As you drive around a typical Florida neighborhood, you will note that it is quite common for the cars to be parked outside. If the garage door is up, you will know why. Garages are the storage space of necessity for those of us that are "over-stuffed."

2. **Plan on a maintenance budget**. In a sub-tropical climate, there are bugs. If your family is like my family, my wife doesn't like bugs in her house. I really don't either. Plan on hiring a regular pest control service. Also, concrete block houses still have wood frame trusses in their roofs, and if you have a frame house, it's all wood. Termites need to be kept at bay. Air Conditioners work hard, plan on replacement anywhere after the ten-year mark. Regular A/C maintenance helps, and the typical A/C has a lifespan of fifteen to eighteen years with some lasting a little longer. Salt spray is in the air, even at a distance from the coast. Corrosion and the need for paint and preservation of metal objects are ever-present. Older homes may be at risk for corrosion of copper piping in their slab foundation. Many older homes have to be re-piped shifting interior water pipes to the attic and down through the walls. It can be an expensive undertaking. Home buyers are well advised to hire a reputable Home Inspector before purchase a new or existing home.

3. **Beware! Be sure you understand your neighborhood's rules**. Deed restrictions and the governance of Home Owners Associations (HOA's) is a fact of life in many of our

neighborhoods. Rules and restrictions vary widely. Be sure you understand the rules of any community you are considering purchasing in. There can be restrictions on pets, pet size, and the number of pets, types of vehicles that can be parked in the neighborhood. There may be requirements that vehicles be parked inside a garage (limiting the size and number of vehicles you can keep on your property,) and we even have some age-restricted communities that restrict ownership to those 55 and older, and the period that any younger family members or friends can stay. An HOA can require a home with inferior maintenance be brought up to neighborhood standards, and they can approve or disapprove exterior changes such as paint colors and landscaping. Home Owner Association rules can be tough, and they are enforced with the full weight of the law.

4. **If you are building a new home, be sure and research any environmental restrictions and construction requirements before purchasing a lot**. The Englewood area and Charlotte County is a good example. There are many vacant lots available at attractive prices. However, protected species such as Scrub Jays and Turtles may spoil your plans and leave you with a lot you can't build on. In many cases, there are remediation measures that can be taken. Be safe, ask before you buy. Be sure you have your builder walk your prospective lot and advise you on any issues you may face. In addition to the environmental concerns, you should ask about construction issues such as the need for expensive fill, and whether the lot is located in a FEMA Flood Zone and therefore requires special flood resistant features and added insurance costs.

5. **If you are buying an older home, check your insurance costs, before you buy.** Florida building codes have evolved over the years. Hurricane disasters have exposed inferior building practices and caused the passage of tougher construction codes. The most recent code update was in 2017 (6th edition.) Home built before then may need retrofitting to obtain the most favorable insurance pricing. The most common retrofits involve adding roof ties to the structural wall and reinforcement of any gable roof ends. Regardless of the age of your prospective home, ask your insurance company and use their expertise.

6. **Investigate the location of Flood Zones and Evacuation Zones that may affect your prospective community.** If you purchase a home and take out a mortgage loan, the lender will require that you purchase Flood Insurance if your property is located in a FEMA Flood Zone. Regardless, any area in Florida is at risk for torrential rains and a local flood event. Flood insurance has its limitations, but it is always advisable, regardless of your home's FEMA Zone designation. County governments also publish their emergency preparedness plans, typically on-line. Many low-lying communities may be subject to evacuation orders in the case of a storm emergency. Learn the requirements for your area, have a storm plan, and identify any evacuation centers you may need. Be sure you know the rules for your pets.

7. **Know your environment.** Alligators are present in canals, ponds and lakes throughout the region. Sharks and alligators may be present in saltwater canals, bays, and even off our beaches. Take care and keep a watchful eye on children and pets especially around the water.

5

Charlotte County, Florida

Single Family Home Sales

Quarterly Median Sale Price & Number of Homes Sold

Trend Lines from 2005 through the First Quarter of 2019

QUARTERLY MEDIAN SALE PRICE Vs SALES VOLUME. SINGLE FAMILY HOMES

Charlotte County, FL

Dollars   Number Sold as Reported in MLS

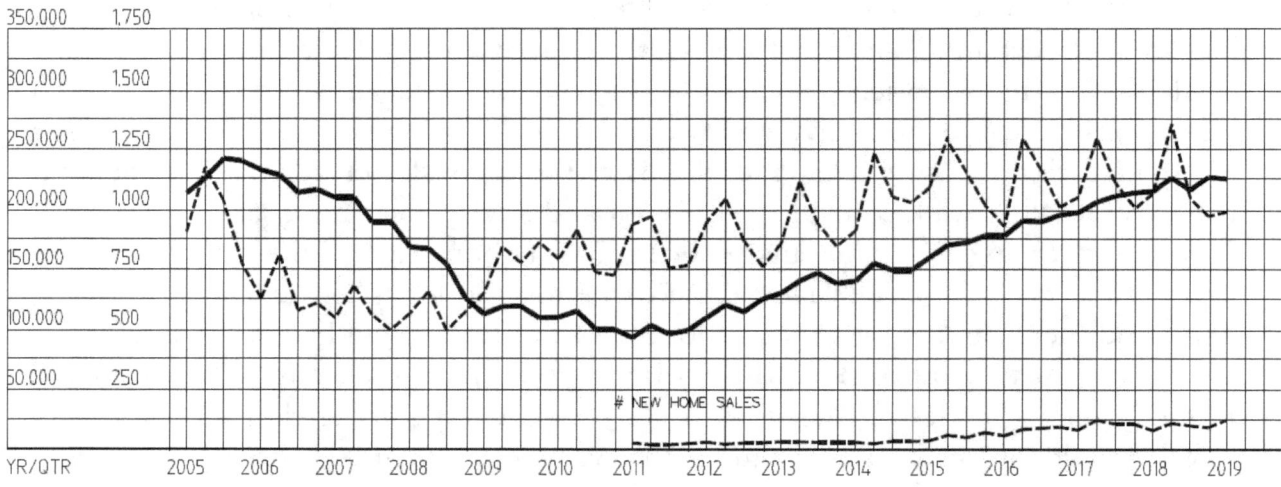

NUMBER SOLD AND MEDIAN SALE PRICE FOR THE PAST EIGHT QUARTERS:

QUARTER	Q2 2017	Q3 2017	Q4 2017	Q1 2018	Q2 2018	Q3 2018	Q4 2018	Q1 2019
# SOLD	1297	1110	1013	1066	1355	1049	971	989
YR/YR 5 QTR # change					58	-61	-42	-77
YR/YR 5 QTR % change					4.47%	-5.50%	-4.15%	-7.22%
$ MEDIAN SALE	206000	211500	213950	215000	226000	216000	227000	225000
4 QTR $ change				9000	14500	2050	12000	-1000
4 QTR % change				4.37%	6.86%	0.96%	5.58%	-0.44%
YR/YR 5 QTR $ change					20000	4500	13050	10000
YR/YR 5 QTR % change					9.71%	2.13%	6.10%	4.65%

The chart illustrates the seasonal and cyclical nature of the Charlotte County market. The typical pattern is rising sales volume and prices in quarters one and two and declining sales volume and softening prices in quarters three and four. The pattern is similar to the seasonal changes in population in the area which sees a large influx of winter residents seeking relief from the cold winters up north. The last major break in the pattern was during the economic downturn that began in 2006 and bottomed in 2011.

Note, the data is from MFR MLS and does not include "By Owner" and direct sales by Auction or by Builder/ Developers.

Charlotte County, Florida

Condominium Sales

Quarterly Median Sale Price & Number of Homes Sold

Trend Lines from 2005 through the First Quarter of 2019

QUARTERLY MEDIAN SALE PRICE Vs SALES VOLUME. CONDOMINIUMS

Charlotte County, FL

Dollars   Number Sold as Reportec in MLS (Villas & Town Homes are not Included)

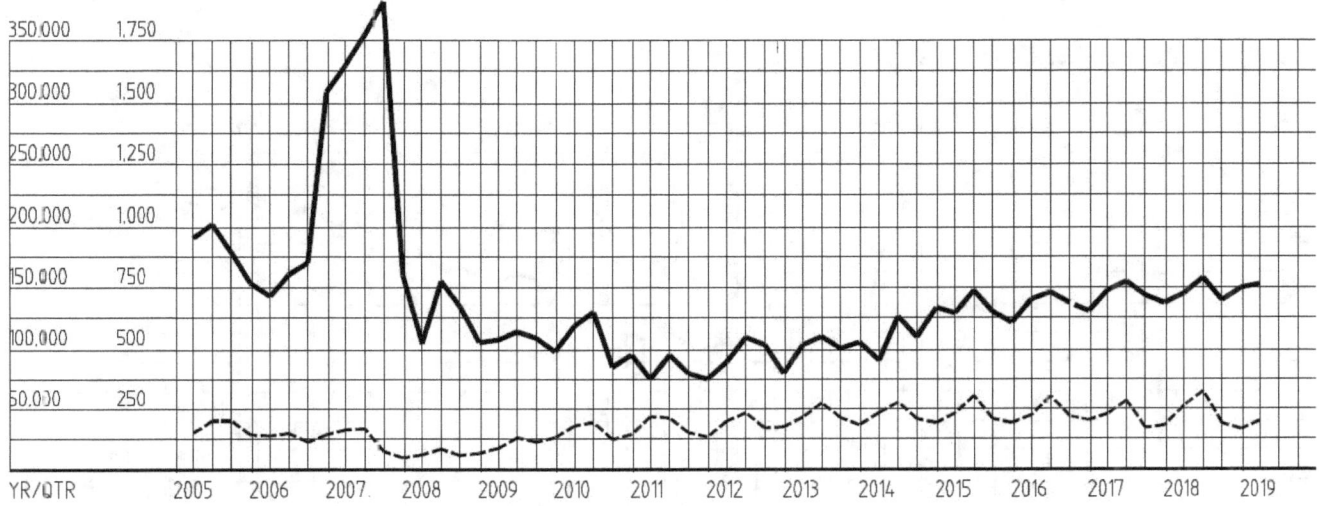

NUMBER SOLD AND MEDIAN SALE PRICE FOR THE PAST EIGHT QUARTERS:

QUARTER	Q2 2017	Q3 2017	Q4 2017	Q1 2018	Q2 2018	Q3 2018	Q4 2018	Q1 2019
# SOLD	**280**	**170**	**179**	**259**	**597**	**187**	**164**	**198**
YR/YR 5 QTR # change					317	17	-15	-61
YR/YR 5 QTR % change					113.21%	10.00%	-8.38%	-23.55%
$ MEDIAN SALE	**154750**	**143000**	**137000**	**145000**	**157500**	**139000**	**149500**	**152700**
4 QTR $ change				-9750	14500	2000	4500	-4800
4 QTR % change				-6.30%	10.14%	1.46%	3.10%	-3.05%
YR/YR 5 QTR $ change					2750	-4000	12500	7700
YR/YR 5 QTR % change					1.78%	-2.80%	9.12%	5.31%

The chart illustrates the seasonal and cyclical nature of the Charlotte County market. The typical pattern is rising sales volume and prices in quarters one and two and declining sales volume and softening prices in quarters three and four. The pattern is similar to the seasonal changes in population in the area which sees a large influx of winter residents seeking relief from the cold winters up north. The last major break in the pattern was during the economic downturn that began in 2006 and bottomed in 2011.

Note, the data is from MFR MLS and does not include "By Owner" and direct sales by Auction or by Builder/ Developers.

Manatee County, Florida

Single Family Home Sales

Quarterly Median Sale Price & Number of Homes Sold

Trend Lines from 2005 through the First Quarter of 2019

QUARTERLY MEDIAN SALE PRICE Vs SALES VOLUME, SINGLE FAMILY HOMES

Manatee County, FL

Dollars   Number Sold as Reported in MLS

NUMBER SOLD AND MEDIAN SALE PRICE FOR THE PAST EIGHT QUARTERS:

QUARTER	Q2 2017	Q3 2017	Q4 2017	Q1 2018	Q2 2018	Q3 2018	Q4 2108	Q1 2109
# SOLD	**1768**	**1541**	**1407**	**1430**	**1881**	**1679**	**1471**	**1376**
YR/YR 5 QTR # change					113	138	64	-54
YR/YR 5 QTR % change					6.39%	8.96%	4.55%	-3.78%
$ MEDIAN SALE	**296500**	**295000**	**299000**	**295000**	**305000**	**299990**	**305000**	**304000**
4 QTR $ change				-1500	10000	990	10000	-1000
4 QTR % change				-0.51%	3.39%	0.33%	3.39%	-0.33%
YR/YR 5 QTR $ change					8500	4990	6000	9000
YR/YR 5 QTR % change					2.87%	1.69%	2.01%	3.05%

The chart illustrates the seasonal and cyclical nature of the Manatee County market. The typical pattern is rising sales volume and prices in quarters one and two and declining sales volume and softening prices in quarters three and four. The pattern is similar to the seasonal changes in population in the area which sees a large influx of winter residents seeking relief from the cold winters up north. The last major break in the pattern was during the economic downturn that began in 2006 and bottomed in 2011.

Note, the data is from MFR MLS and does not include "By Owner" and direct sales by Auction or by Builder/Developers.

Manatee County, Florida

Condominium Sales

Quarterly Median Sale Price & Number of Homes Sold

Trend Lines from 2005 through the First Quarter of 2019

QUARTERLY MEDIAN SALE PRICE Vs SALES VOLUME. CONDOMINIUMS

Manatee County, FL

Dollars   Number Sold as Reported in MLS (Villas & Town Homes are not Included)

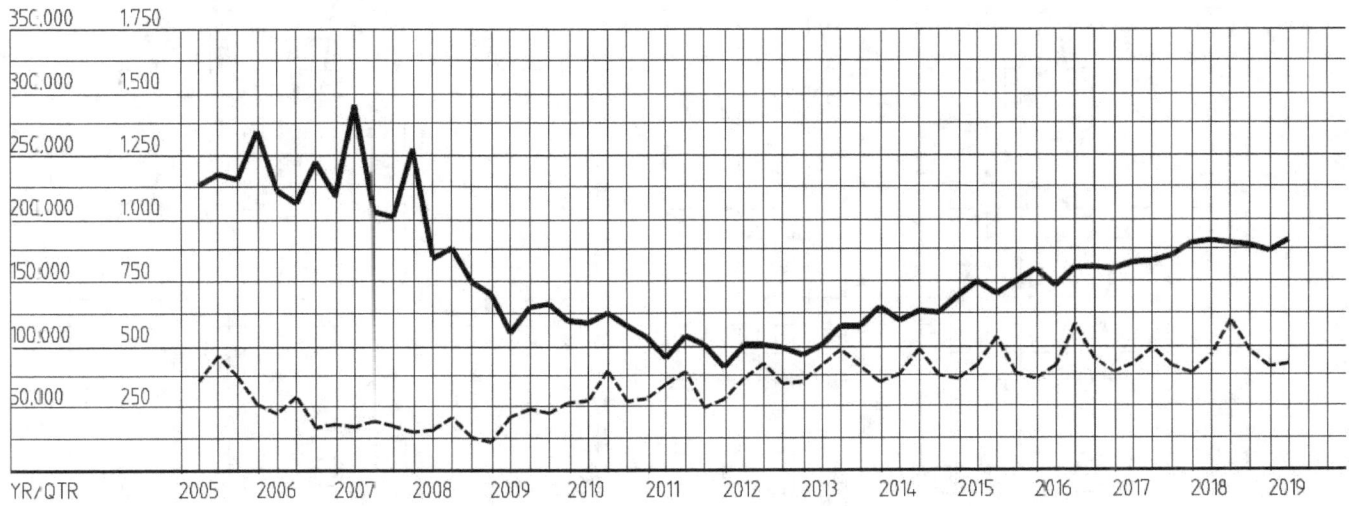

NUMBER SOLD AND MEDIAN SALE PRICE FOR THE PAST EIGHT QUARTERS:

QUARTER	Q2 2017	Q3 2017	Q4 2017	Q1 2018	Q2 2018	Q3 2018	Q4 2018	Q1 2019
# SOLD	490	415	385	458	597	474	409	423
YR/YR 5 QTR # change					107	59	24	-35
YR/YR 5 QTR % change					21.84%	14.22%	6.23%	-7.64%
$ MEDIAN SALE	165850	170000	180000	181999	180000	178500	173500	182500
4 QTR $ change				16149	10000	-1500	-8499	2500
4 QTR % change				9.74%	5.88%	-0.83%	-4.67%	1.39%
YR/YR 5 QTR $ change					14150	8500	-6500	501
YR/YR 5 QTR % change					8.53%	5.00%	-3.61%	0.28%

The chart illustrates the seasonal and cyclical nature of the Manatee County market. The typical pattern is rising sales volume and prices in quarters one and two and declining sales volume and softening prices in quarters three and four. The pattern is similar to the seasonal changes in population in the area which sees a large influx of winter residents seeking relief from the cold winters up north. The last major break in the pattern was during the economic downturn that began in 2006 and bottomed in 2011.

Note, the data is from MFR MLS and does not include "By Owner" and direct sales by Auction or by Builder/ Developers.

Sarasota County, Florida

Single Family Home Sales

Quarterly Median Sale Price & Number of Homes Sold

Trend Lines from 2005 through the First Quarter of 2019

QUARTERLY MEDIAN SALE PRICE Vs SALES VOLUME. SINGLE FAMILY HOMES

Sarasota County, FL

Dollars Number Sold as Reported in MLS

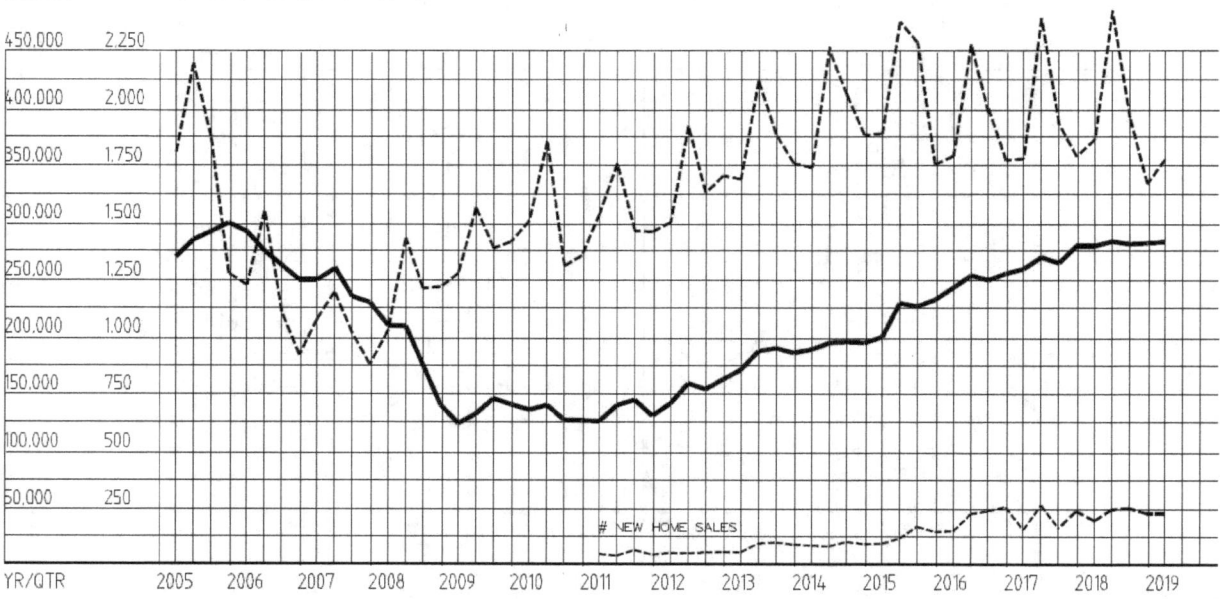

NUMBER SOLD AND MEDIAN SALE PRICE FOR THE PAST EIGHT QUARTERS:

QUARTER	Q2 2017	Q3 2017	Q4 2017	Q1 2018	Q2 2018	Q3 2018	Q4 2018	Q1 2019
# SOLD	**2391**	**1932**	**1792**	**1867**	**2426**	**1960**	**1669**	**1778**
YR/YR 5 QTR # change					35	28	-123	-89
YR/YR 5 QTR % change					1.46%	1.45%	-6.86%	-4.77%
$ MEDIAN SALE	**270000**	**265000**	**280000**	**280000**	**283793**	**281250**	**282500**	**283500**
4 QTR $ change				10000	18793	1250	2500	-293
4 QTR % change				3.70%	7.09%	0.45%	0.89%	-0.10%
YR/YR 5 QTR $ change					13793	16250	2500	3500
YR/YR 5 QTR % change					5.11%	6.13%	0.89%	1.25%

The chart illustrates the seasonal and cyclical nature of the Sarasota County market. The typical pattern is rising sales volume and prices in quarters one and two and declining sales volume and softening prices in quarters three and four. The pattern is similar to the seasonal changes in population in the area which sees a large influx of winter residents seeking relief from the cold winters up north. The last major break in the pattern was during the economic downturn that began in 2006 and bottomed in 2011.

Note, the data is from MFR MLS and does not include "By Owner" and direct sales by Auction or by Builder/Developers.

Sarasota County, Florida

Condominium Sales

Quarterly Median Sale Price & Number of Homes Sold

Trend Lines from 2005 through the First Quarter of 2019

QUARTERLY MEDIAN SALE PRICE Vs SALES VOLUME, CONDOMINIUMS

Sarasota County, FL

Dollars   Number Sold in MLS (Villas & Town Homes are not Included)

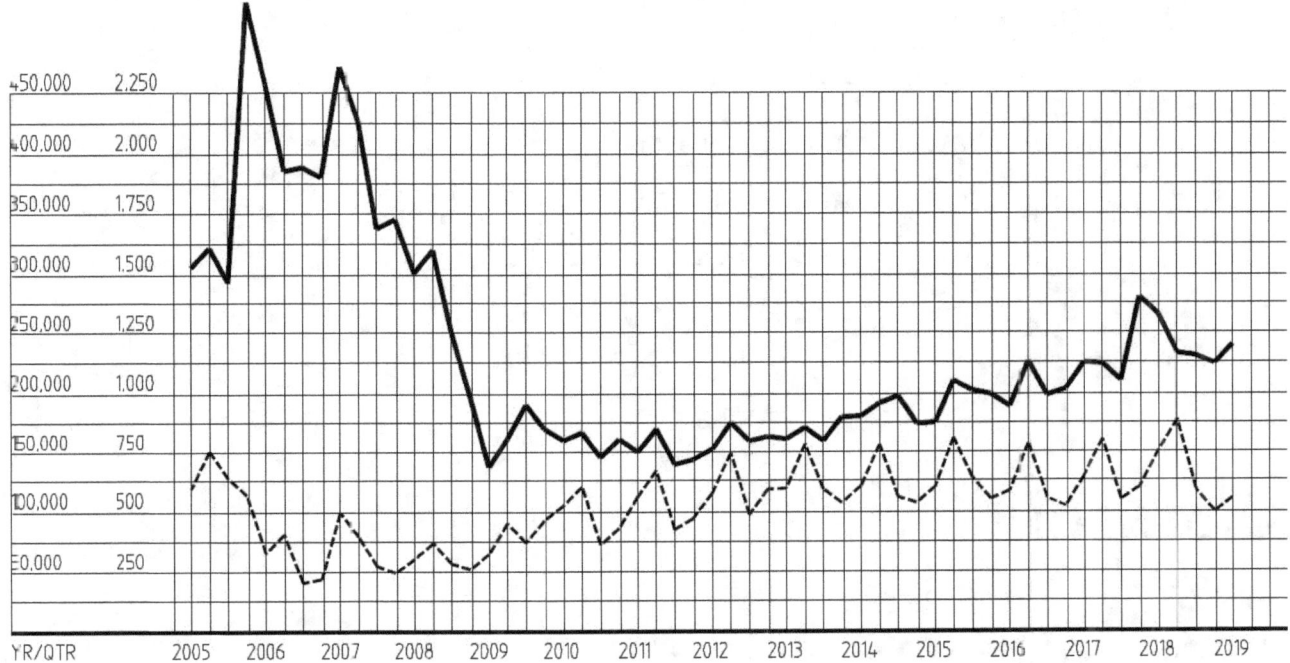

NUMBER SOLD AND MEDIAN SALE PRICE FOR THE PAST EIGHT QUARTERS:

QUARTER	Q2 2017	Q3 2017	Q4 2017	Q1 2018	Q2 2018	Q3 2018	Q4 2018	Q1 2019
# SOLD	802	546	598	754	889	584	495	551
YR/YR 5 QTR # change					87	38	-103	-203
YR/YR 5 QTR % change					10.85%	6.96%	-17.22%	-26.92%
$ MEDIAN SALE	223750	210000	280250	265000	232500	230500	224000	240000
4 QTR $ change				41250	22500	-49750	-41000	7500
4 QTR % change				18.44%	10.71%	-17.75%	-15.47%	3.23%
YR/YR 5 QTR $ change					8750	20500	-56250	-25000
YR/YR 5 QTR % change					3.91%	9.76%	-20.07%	-9.43%

The chart illustrates the seasonal and cyclical nature of the Sarasota County market. The typical pattern is rising sales volume and prices in quarters one and two and declining sales volume and softening prices in quarters three and four. The pattern is similar to the seasonal changes in population in the area which sees a large influx of winter residents seeking relief from the cold winters up north. The last major break in the pattern was during the economic downturn that began in 2006 and bottomed in 2011.

Note, the data is from MFR MLS and does not include "By Owner" and direct sales by Auction or by Builder/ Developers.

BRADENTON

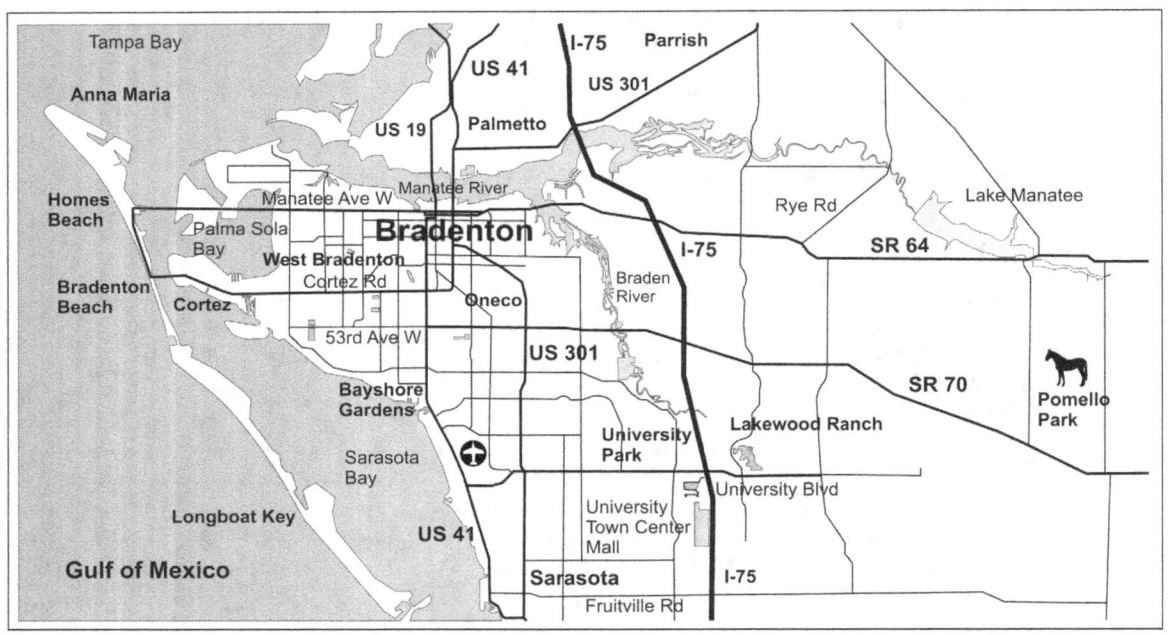

BRADENTON

Single Family Home Sales

Q1 2019 Buying Power Chart

Market Segment - Median:	Price $	Bed	Bath	Sq Ft Heated
Top Sale - maximum	3,000,000	6	7	8143
Upper 1/16	647,500	3	4	2906
Upper 1/8	526,000	3	3	2689
Upper 1/4	410,000	3	3	2371
Median	299,900	3	2	1887
Lower 1/4	225,870	3	2	1544
Lower1/8	175,000	3	2	1272
Lower 1/16	155,000	3	2	1135
Low Sale - minimum	40,000	2	1	648

Bradenton Q2 2017 to Q1 2019

SINGLE FAMILY HOME SALES

QUARTER	Q2 2017	Q3 2017	Q4 2017	Q1 2018	Q2 2018	Q3 2018	Q4 2018	Q1 2019
# SOLD	909	790	719	750	980	865	775	711
YR/YR 5 QTR # CHANGE					71	75	56	-39
YR/YR 5 QTR % CHANGE					7.81%	9.49%	7.79%	-5.20%
$ MEDIAN SALE	285000	285000	291000	279950	295000	290000	297990	299900
4 QTR $ CHANGE				-5050	10000	-1000	18040	4900
4 QTR % CHANGE				-1.77%	3.51%	-0.34%	6.44%	1.66%
YR/YR 5 QTR $ CHANGE					10000	5000	6990	19950
YR/YR 5 QTR % CHANGE					3.51%	1.75%	2.40%	7.13%
MID-RANGE SALES:								
$ LOWER 1/4	213000	206500	215000	209000	229900	219995	216200	225870
$ UPPER 1/4	379887	384563	398000	395000	404000	399700	408484	410000
$ HIGH SALE	3495000	2275000	3500000	2350000	1900000	4600000	2350000	3000000

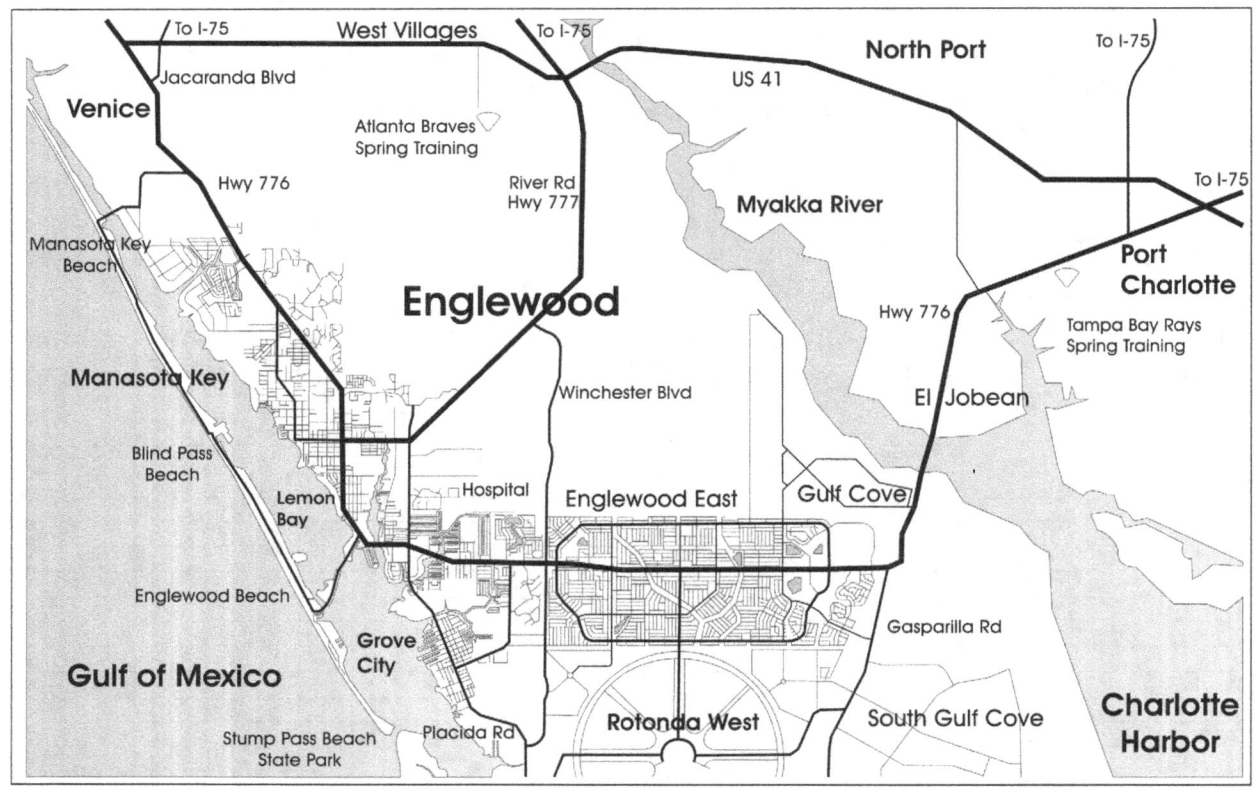

ENGLEWOOD

Single Family Home Sales

Q1 2019 Buying Power Chart

Market Segment- Median:	Price $	Bed	Bath	Sq Ft Heated
Top Sale - maximum	3,050,000	6	6	6546
Upper 1/16	604,000	3	3	2815
Upper 1/8	427,500	3	2	2339
Upper 1/4	329,000	3	2	1969
Median	230,000	3	2	1636
Lower 1/4	175,000	2	2	1269
Lower1/8	150,000	2	2	1056
Lower 1/16	132,000	2	2	1008
Low Sale - minimum	64,200	1	1	400

Englewood Q2 2017— Q1 2019

SINGLE FAMILY HOME SALES

QUARTER	Q2 2017	Q3 2017	Q4 2017	Q1 2018	Q2 2018	Q3 2018	Q4 2018	Q1 2019
# SOLD	216	170	156	188	242	165	157	173
YR/YR 5 QTR # CHANGE					26	-5	1	-15
YR/YR 5 QTR % CHANGE					12.04%	-2.94%	0.64%	-7.98%
$ MEDIAN SALE	223500	225000	215000	236550	244250	222000	230000	230000
4 QTR $ CHANGE				13050	19250	7000	-6550	-14250
4 QTR % CHANGE				5.84%	8.56%	3.26%	-2.77%	-5.83%
YR/YR 5 QTR $ CHANGE					20750	-3000	15000	-6550
YR/YR 5 QTR % CHANGE					9.28%	-1.33%	6.98%	-2.77%
MID-RANGE SALES:								
$ LOWER 1/4	152000	166000	160000	170000	185000	179000	184500	175000
$ UPPER 1/4	300000	304019	300000	332750	321000	309900	314664	329000
$ HIGH SALE	3500000	3250000	1200000	2300000	4650000	3000000	1700000	3050000

GULF COVE & SOUTH GULF COVE

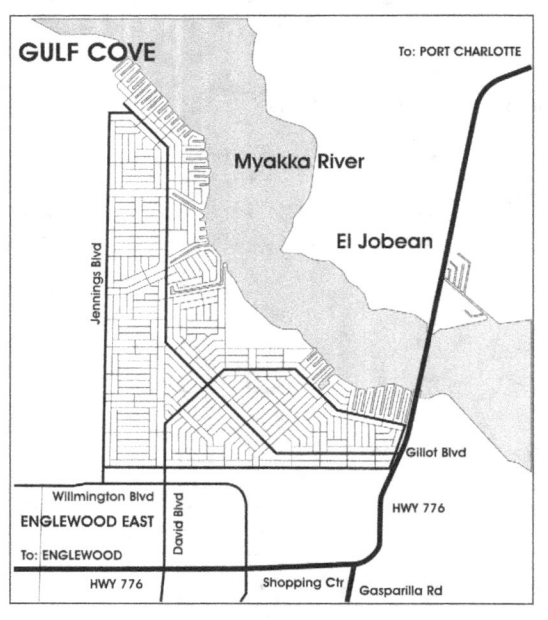

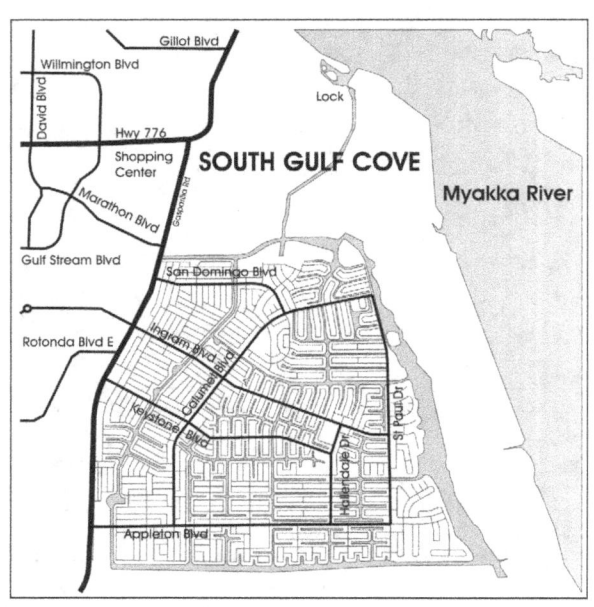

GULF COVE - SOUTH GULF COVE

Single Family Home Sales

Q1 2019 Buying Power Chart

Market Segment - Median:	Price		Bed	Bath	Sq Ft Heated
Top Sale - maximum	$	680,000	6	5	3896
Upper 1/16	$	483,500	3	2	2321
Upper 1/8	$	410,000	3	2	2175
Upper 1/4	$	375,500	3	2	2135
Median	$	270,000	3	2	1841
Lower 1/4	$	205,000	3	2	1540
Lower1/8	$	169,150	3	2	1333
Lower 1/16	$	150,000	3	2	1296
Low Sale - minimum	$	111,000	2	1	918

Gulf Cove & South Gulf Cove Q2 2017— Q1 2019

SINGLE FAMILY HOME SALES

QUARTER	Q2 2017	Q3 2017	Q4 2017	Q1 2018	Q2 2018	Q3 2018	Q4 2108	Q1 2109
# SOLD	104	105	90	85	106	79	85	89
YR/YR 5 QTR # CHANGE					2	-26	-5	4
YR/YR 5 QTR % CHANGE					1.92%	-24.76%	-5.56%	4.71%
$ MEDIAN SALE	242500	279000	259700	261800	256500	286000	283205	270000
4 QTR $ CHANGE				19300	-22500	26300	21405	13500
4 QTR % CHANGE				7.96%	-8.06%	10.13%	8.18%	5.26%
YR/YR 5 QTR $ CHANGE					14000	7000	23505	8200
YR/YR 5 QTR % CHANGE					5.77%	2.51%	9.05%	3.13%
MID-RANGE SALES:								
$ LOWER 1/4	175000	213400	180000	165500	192000	181500	188000	205000
$ UPPER 1/4	383500	381777	385000	381500	400000	392000	374400	375500
$ HIGH SALE	675000	959300	942786	675000	950000	1400000	800000	680000

YR/QTR. ENDING: 1st 2017   2nd   3rd   4th   1st 2018   2nd   3rd   4th   1st 2019

LAKEWOOD RANCH

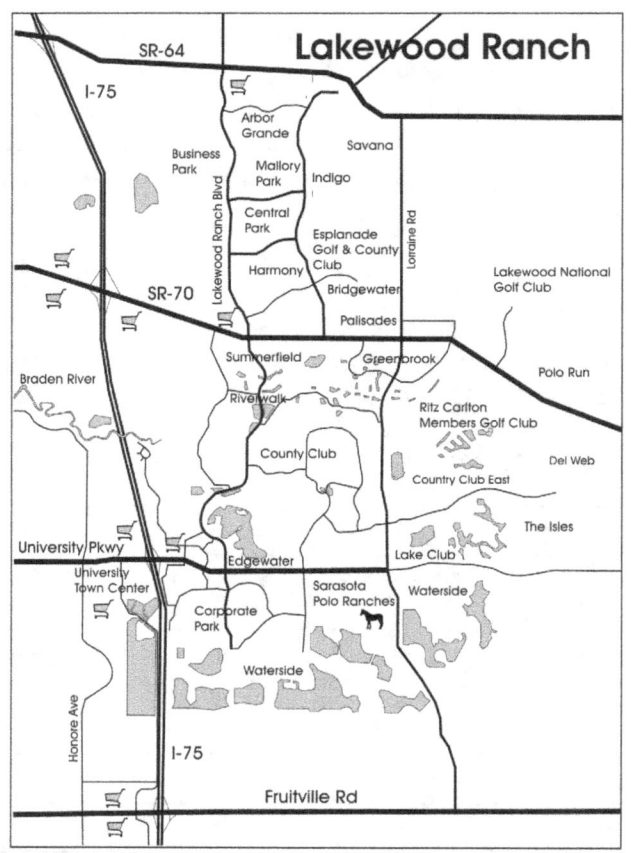

LAKEWOOD RANCH

Single Family Home Sales

Q1 2019 Buying Power Chart

Market Segment - Median:	Price	Bed	Bath	Sq Ft Heated
Top Sale - maximum	$ 2,500,000	6	6	7364
Upper 1/16	$ 1,270,000	3	5	3787
Upper 1/8	$ 1,115,000	3	4	3687
Upper 1/4	$ 699,500	3	3	3270
Median	$ 510,000	3	3	2488
Lower 1/4	$ 352,400	3	2	1981
Lower 1/8	$ 300,000	3	2	1884
Lower 1/16	$ 270,000	3	2	1696
Low Sale - minimum	$ 229,000	2	2	1156

Lakewood Ranch Q2 2017—Q1 2019

SINGLE FAMILY HOME SALES

QUARTER	Q2 2017	Q3 2017	Q4 2017	Q1 2018	Q2 2018	Q3 2018	Q4 2018	Q1 2019
# SOLD	153	143	131	126	185	145	118	107
YR/YR 5 QTR # CHANGE					32	2	-13	-19
YR/YR 5 QTR % CHANGE					20.92%	1.40%	-9.92%	-15.08%
$ MEDIAN SALE	393098	412000	425000	448000	430000	430590	493000	510000
4 QTR $ CHANGE				54902	18000	5590	45000	80000
4 QTR % CHANGE				13.97%	4.37%	1.32%	10.04%	18.60%
YR/YR 5 QTR $ CHANGE					36902	18590	68000	62000
YR/YR 5 QTR % CHANGE					9.39%	4.51%	16.00%	13.84%
MID-RANGE SALES:								
$ LOWER 1/4	315000	305000	322530	325000	339000	355000	380000	352400
$ UPPER 1/4	510000	550000	589500	595000	595000	619000	701000	699500
$ HIGH SALE	1799327	1695000	2050000	1645000	3160000	1550000	2125000	2500000
$ UPPER 1/16	843000	943244	1175000	1124525	132500	1125000	1275000	1270000
$ UPPER 1/8								1115000

NOKOMIS, NORTH VENICE, OSPREY

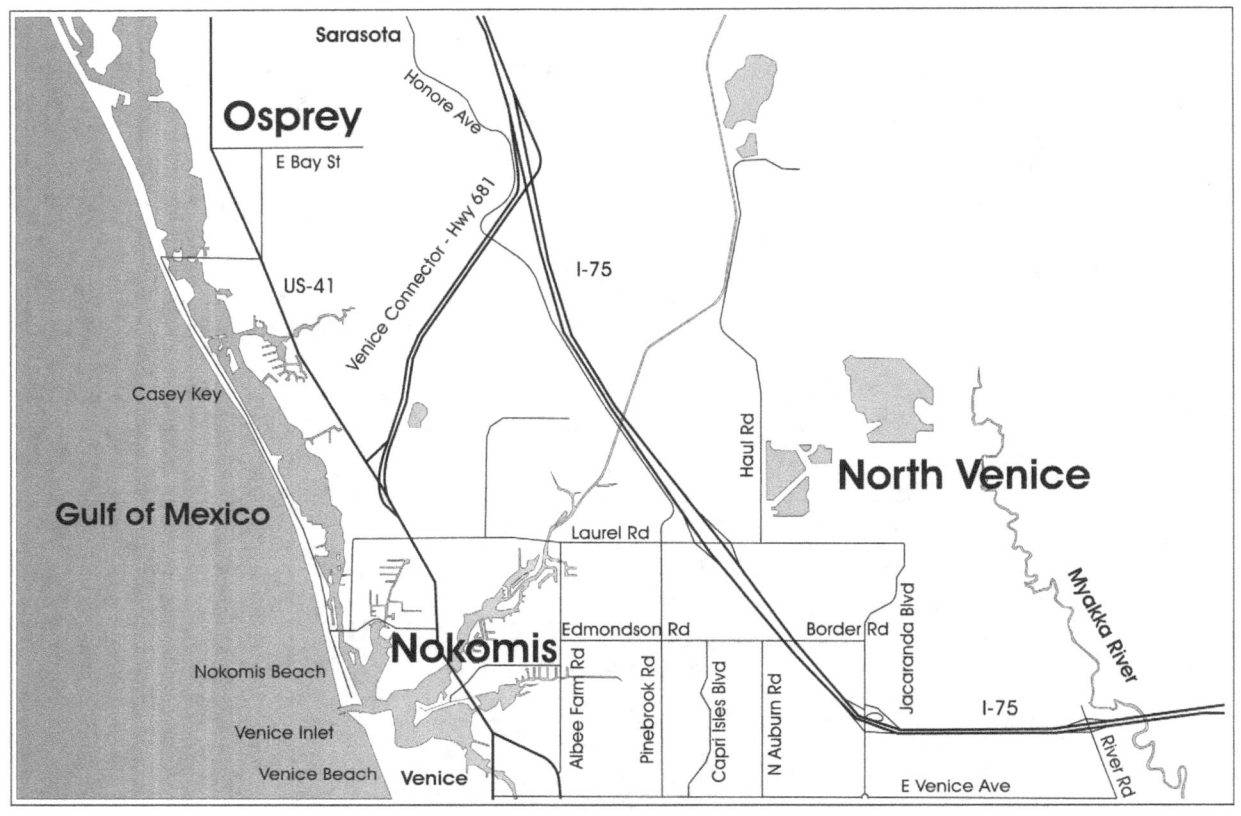

NOKOMIS, NORTH VENICE, OSPREY

Single Family Home Sales

Q1 2019 Buying Power Chart

Market Segment - Median:	Price	Bed	Bath	Sq Ft Heated
Top Sale - maximum	$ 5,300,000	7	10	6861
Upper 1/16	$ 1,400,000	4	4	4172
Upper 1/8	$ 750,000	4	4	3658
Upper 1/4	$ 520,000	3	3	2763
Median	$ 413,000	3	2	2100
Lower 1/4	$ 319,500	3	2	1810
Lower 1/8	$ 256,000	3	2	1519
Lower 1/16	$ 195,000	2	2	1272
Low Sale - minimum	$ 60,000	2	1	902

Nokomis, North Venice, Osprey Q2 2017— Q1 2019

SINGLE FAMILY HOME SALES:

QUARTER	Q2 2017	Q3 2017	Q4 2017	Q1 2018	Q2 2018	Q3 2018	Q4 2108	Q1 2109
# SOLD	207	156	142	163	187	165	142	131
YR/YR 5 QTR # CHANGE					-20	9	0	-32
YR/YR 5 QTR % CHANGE					-9.66%	5.77%	0.00%	-19.63%
$ MEDIAN SALE	385000	359950	364000	370000	378000	379900	365781	413000
4 QTR $ CHANGE				-15000	18050	15900	-4219	35000
4 QTR % CHANGE				-3.90%	5.01%	4.37%	-1.14%	9.26%
YR/YR 5 QTR $ CHANGE					-7000	19950	1781	43000
YR/YR 5 QTR % CHANGE					-1.82%	5.54%	0.49%	11.62%

MID-RANGE SALES:

	Q2 2017	Q3 2017	Q4 2017	Q1 2018	Q2 2018	Q3 2018	Q4 2108	Q1 2109
$ LOWER 1/4	309941	295000	304990	287303	305450	300000	270088	319500
$ UPPER 1/4	502500	565000	500170	510000	520000	475000	460000	520000
$ HIGH SALE	4350000	6550000	3100000	3250000	4500000	4000000	6100000	5300000
$ UPPER 1/16	860000	1160000	780000	1000000	1007500	670000	1250000	1400000

| YR./QTR. ENDING: | 1st 2017 | 2nd | 3rd | 4th | 1st 2018 | 2nd | 3rd | 4th | 1st 2019 |

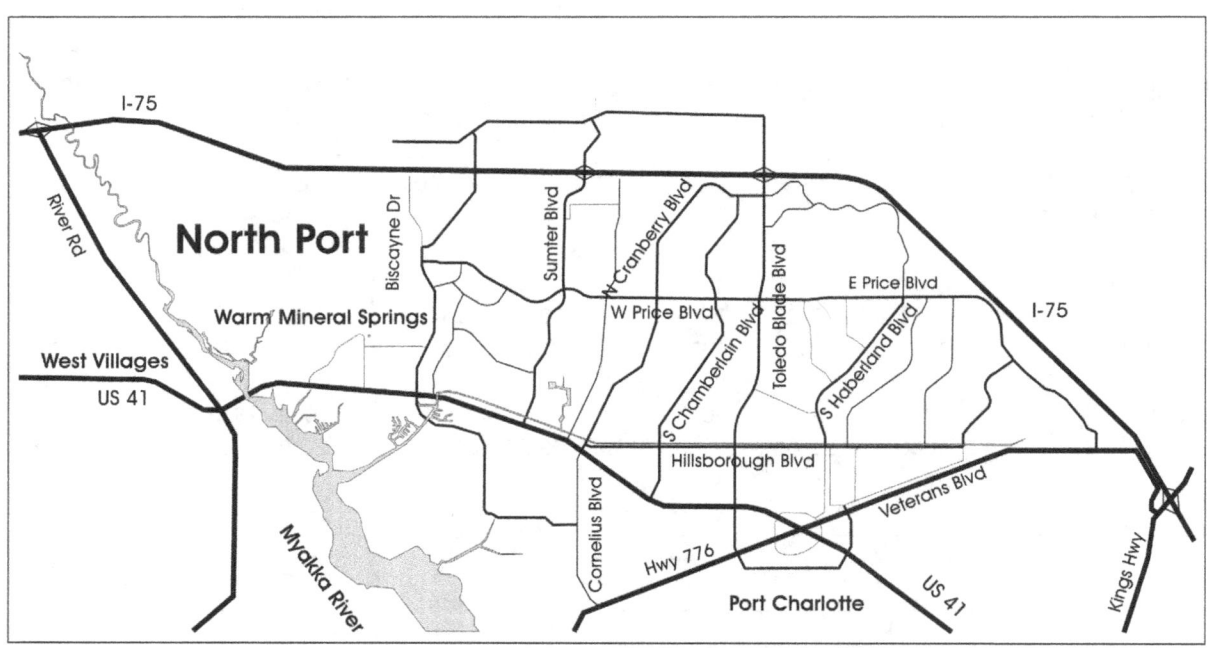

NORTH PORT

Single Family Home Sales

Q1 2019 Buying Power Chart

Market Segment - Median:	Price	Bed	Bath	Sq Ft Heated
Top Sale - maximum	$ 560,000	6	4	4162
Upper 1/16	$ 315,000	3	2	2243
Upper 1/8	$ 285,000	3	2	2047
Upper 1/4	$ 246,000	3	2	1819
Median	$ 206,900	3	2	1592
Lower 1/4	$ 174,000	3	2	1320
Lower1/8	$ 150,000	3	2	1203
Lower 1/16	$ 130,000	2	2	1117
Low Sale - minimum	$ 50,000	1	1	588

North Port Q2 2017—Q1 2019

SINGLE FAMILY HOME SALES

QUARTER	Q2 2017	Q3 2017	Q4 2017	Q1 2018	Q2 2018	Q3 2018	Q4 2108	Q1 2109
# SOLD	533	428	387	402	491	434	343	391
YR/YR 5 QTR # CHANGE					-42	6	-44	-11
YR/YR 5 QTR % CHANGE					-7.88%	1.40%	-11.37%	-2.74%
$ MEDIAN SALE	189900	190250	191650	200450	206000	205000	208000	206900
4 QTR $ CHANGE				10550	15750	13350	7550	900
4 QTR % CHANGE				5.56%	8.28%	6.97%	3.77%	0.44%
YR/YR 5 QTR $ CHANGE					16100	14750	16350	6450
YR/YR 5 QTR % CHANGE					8.48%	7.75%	8.53%	3.22%
MID-RANGE SALES:								
$ LOWER 1/4	164000	157000	164700	170000	175000	172700	175500	174000
$ UPPER 1/4	236000	229450	235250	239500	245150	235500	250000	246000
$ HIGH SALE	512000	480000	828000	557500	715000	475000	469000	560000

| YR/QTR. ENDING: | 1st 2017 | 2nd | 3rd | 4th | 1st 2018 | 2nd | 3rd | 4th | 1st 2019 |

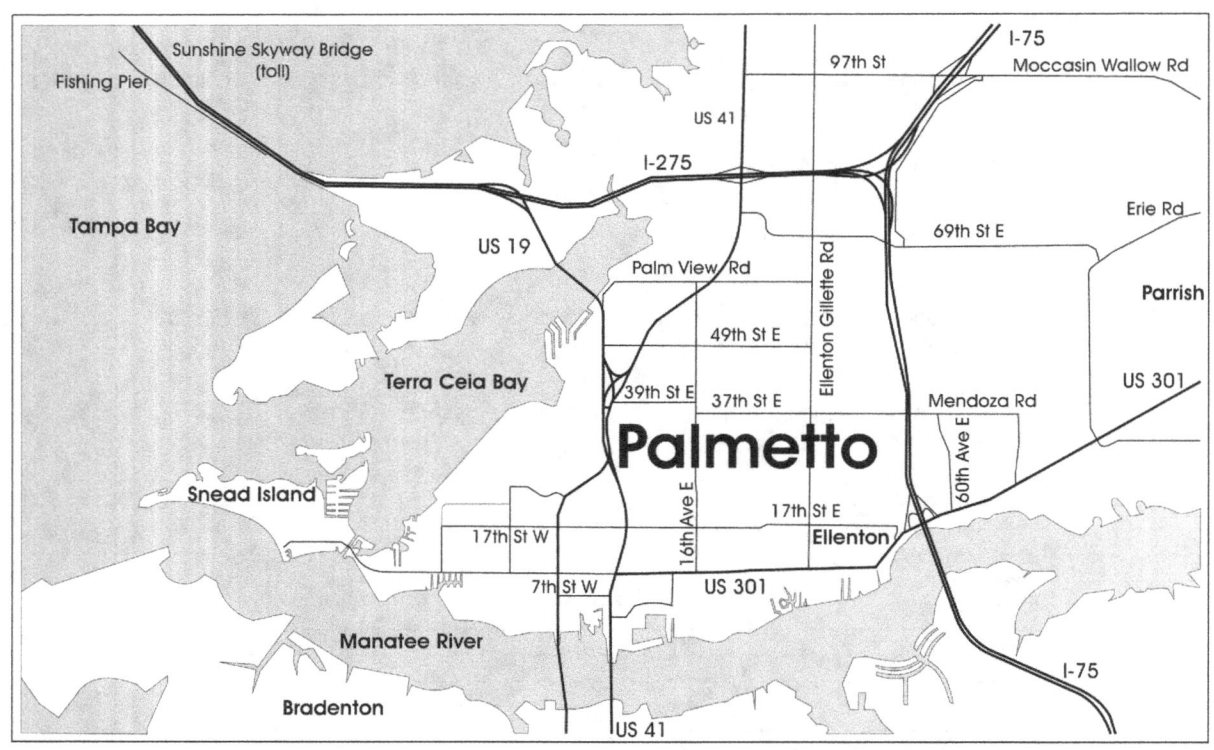

PALMETTO

Single Family Home Sales

Q1 2019 Buying Power Chart

Market Segment - Median:	Price	Bed	Bath	Sq Ft Heated
Top Sale - maximum	$ 1,250,000	5	5	3832
Upper 1/16	$ 513,603	3	3	2645
Upper 1/8	$ 374,767	3	3	2478
Upper 1/4	$ 300,000	4	3	2285
Median	$ 254,099	3	2	1847
Lower 1/4	$ 214,495	3	2	1504
Lower1/8	$ 189,000	3	2	1311
Lower 1/16	$ 169,000	3	2	1223
Low Sale - minimum	$ 51,000	2	1	780

Palmetto Q2 2017—Q1 2019

SINGLE FAMILY HOME SALES

QUARTER	Q2 2017	Q3 2017	Q4 2017	Q1 2018	Q2 2018	Q3 2018	Q4 2018	Q1 2019
# SOLD	203	183	167	161	198	204	170	204
YR/YR 5 QTR # CHANGE					-5	21	3	43
YR/YR 5 QTR % CHANGE					-2.46%	11.48%	1.80%	26.71%
$ MEDIAN SALE	225000	234990	243000	232787	247706	249450	246613	254099
4 QTR $ CHANGE				7787	12716	6450	13826	6393
4 QTR % CHANGE				3.46%	5.41%	2.65%	5.94%	2.58%
YR/YR 5 QTR $ CHANGE					22706	14460	3613	21312
YR/YR 5 QTR % CHANGE					10.09%	6.15%	1.49%	9.16%
MID-RANGE SALES:								
$ LOWER 1/4	189800	202000	196500	200000	209850	215000	208000	214495
$ UPPER 1/4	264265	276925	386995	286990	295550	279450	299000	300000
$ HIGH SALE	825000	1610000	1750000	1225000	1785000	810000	2400000	1250000

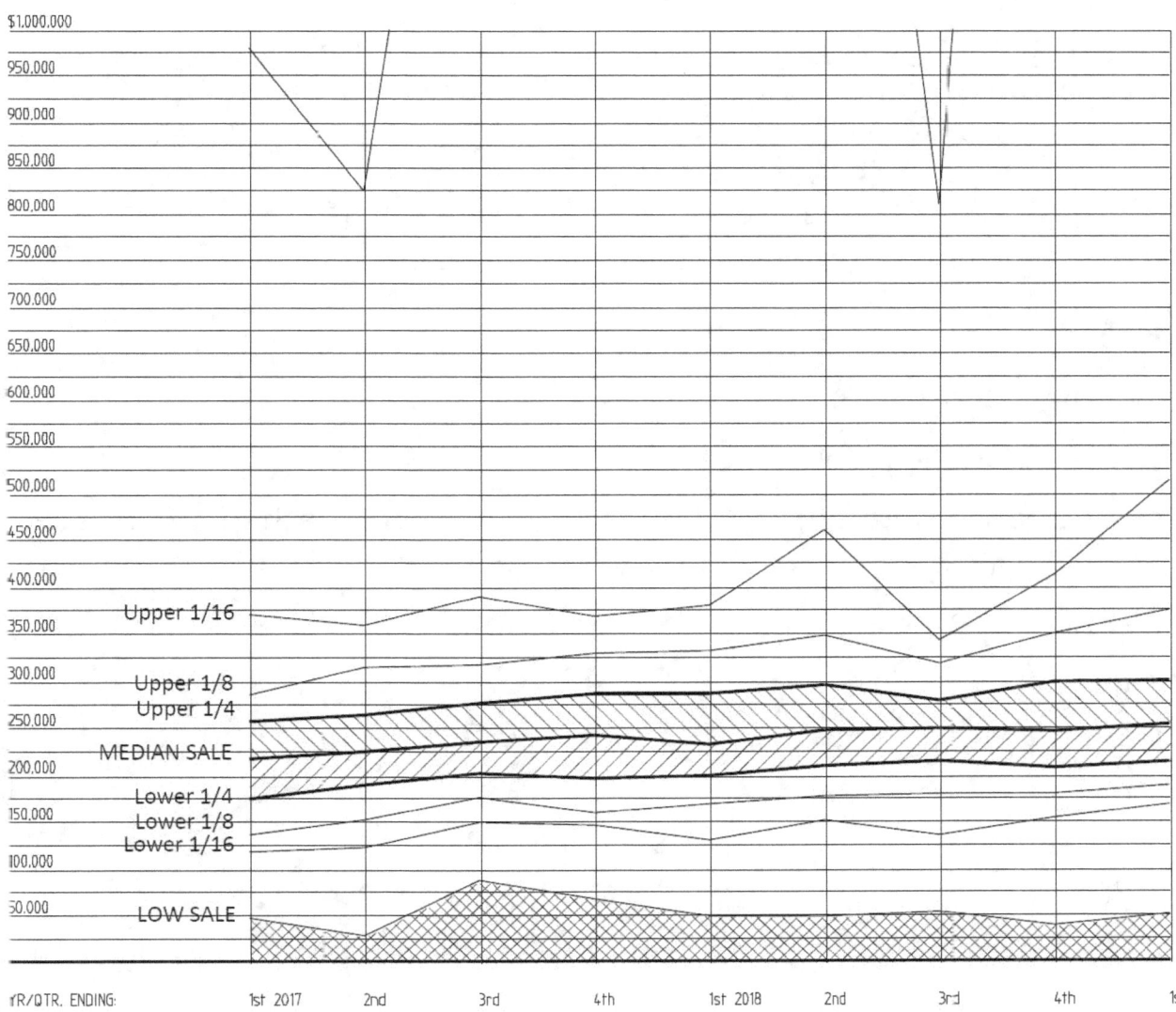

PARRISH

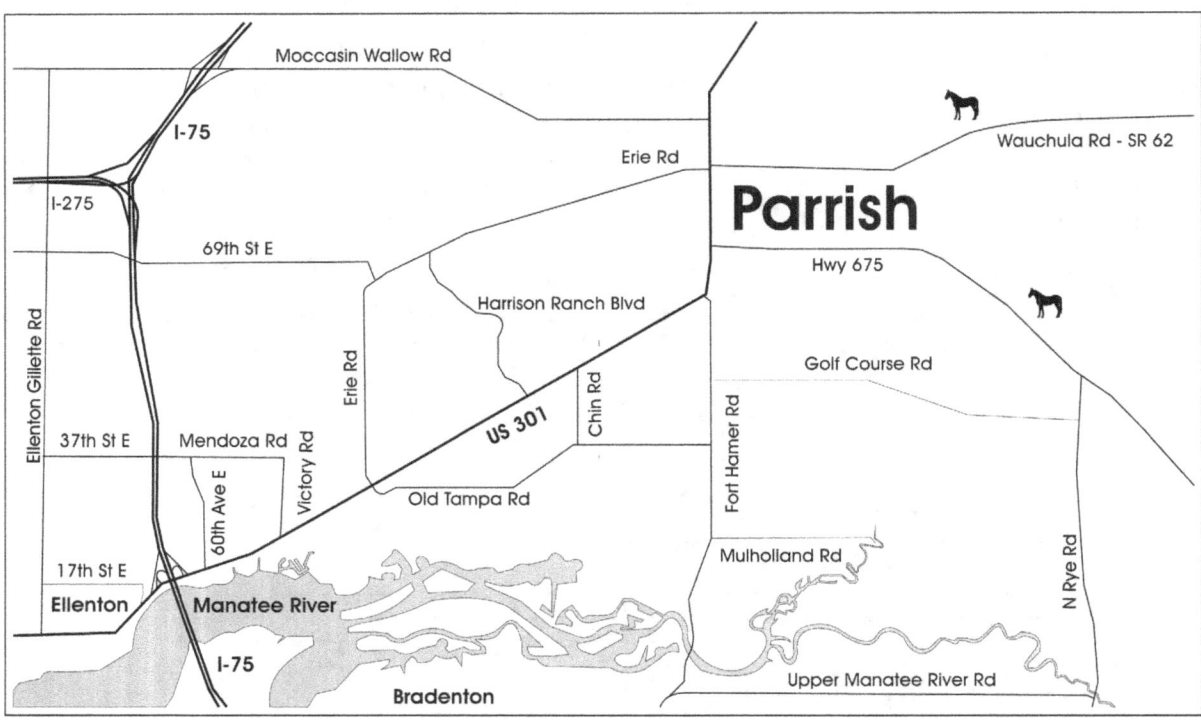

PARRISH

Single Family Home Sales

Q1 2019 Buying Power Chart

Market Segment - Median:	Price	Bed	Bath	Sq Ft Heated
Top Sale - maximum	$ 1,325,000	6	5	4563
Upper 1/16	$ 504,500	3	3	3224
Upper 1/8	$ 455,000	3	3	3056
Upper 1/4	$ 381,250	3	3	2732
Median	$ 299,950	3	2	2164
Lower 1/4	$ 254,948	3	2	1862
Lower1/8	$ 240,000	3	2	1599
Lower 1/16	$ 230,000	3	2	1488
Low Sale - minimum	$ 155,000	2	1	704

Parrish Q2 2017—Q1 2019

SINGLE FAMILY HOME SALES

QUARTER	Q2 2017	Q3 2017	Q4 2017	Q1 2018	Q2 2018	Q3 2018	Q4 2108	Q1 2109
# SOLD	179	158	147	130	167	189	165	140
YR/YR 5 QTR # CHANGE					-12	31	18	10
YR/YR 5 QTR % CHANGE					-6.70%	19.62%	12.24%	7.69%
$ MEDIAN SALE	279900	291120	285000	302500	275000	286000	298000	299950
4 QTR $ CHANGE				22600	-16120	1000	-4500	24950
4 QTR % CHANGE				8.07%	-5.54%	0.35%	-1.49%	9.07%
YR/YR 5 QTR $ CHANGE					-4900	-5120	13000	-2550
YR/YR 5 QTR % CHANGE					-1.75%	-1.76%	4.56%	-0.84%
MID-RANGE SALES:								
$ LOWER 1/4	240000	246000	245000	257000	250000	257500	257000	254948
$ UPPER 1/4	340545	350000	339950	375000	343250	359000	355000	381250
$ HIGH SALE	750000	1155000	945717	698000	899000	1550000	850000	1325000

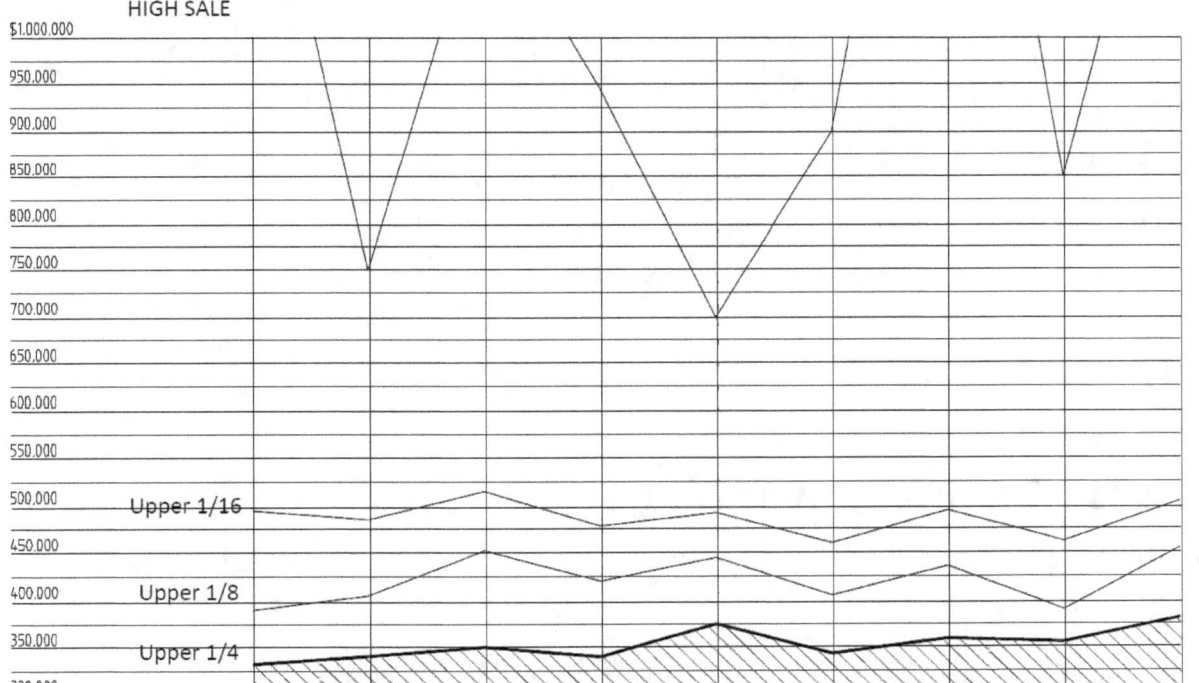

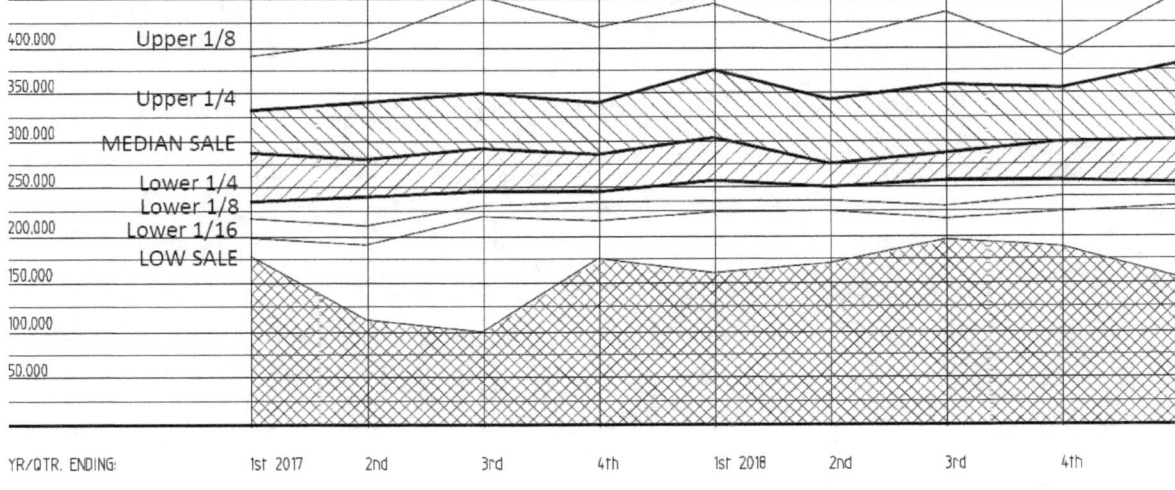

PORT CHARLOTTE

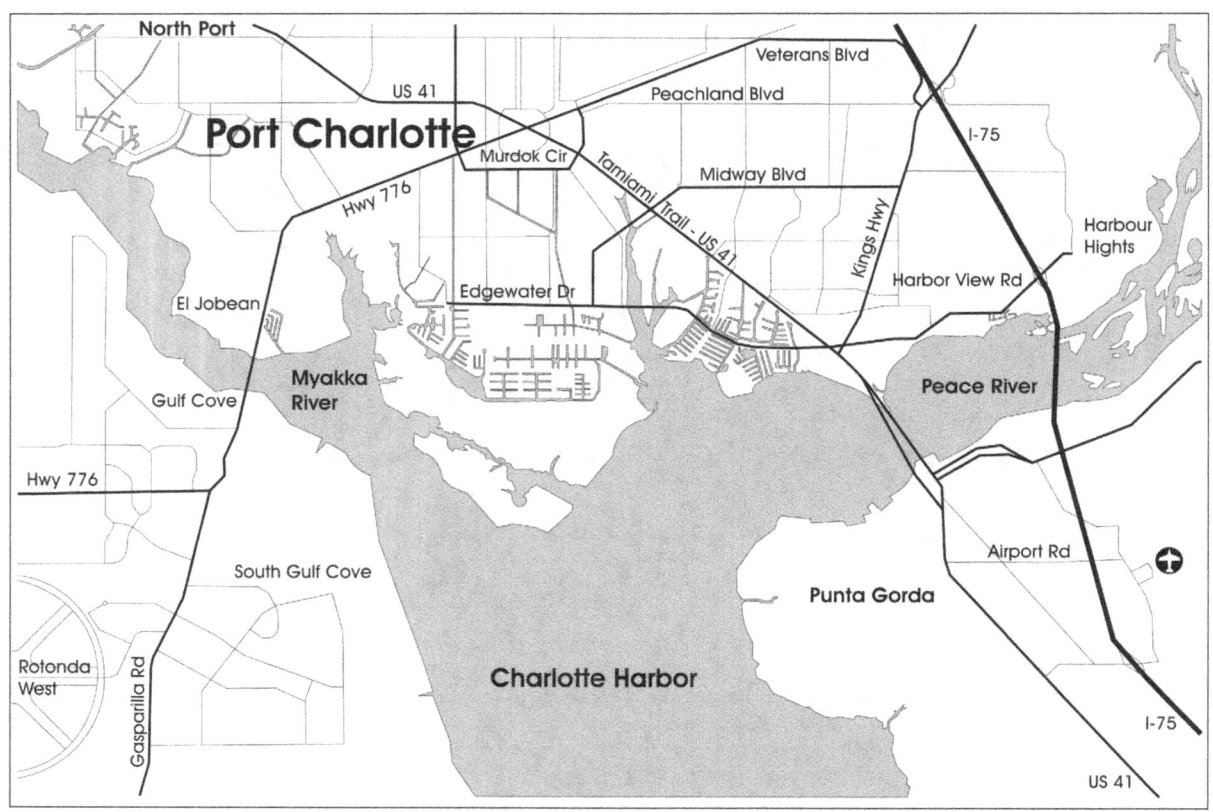

PORT CHARLOTTE

Single Family Home Sales

Q1 2019 Buying Power Chart

Market Segment - Median:	Price	Bed	Bath	Sq Ft Heated
Top Sale - maximum	$ 916,500	6	5	4444
Upper 1/16	$ 395,000	3	2	2175
Upper 1/8	$ 329,100	3	2	2082
Upper 1/4	$ 267,500	3	2	1893
Median	$ 190,000	3	2	1578
Lower 1/4	$ 152,000	3	2	1320
Lower 1/8	$ 125,000	2	2	1140
Lower 1/16	$ 110,750	2	2	1124
Low Sale - minimum	$ 65,100	1	1	525

Port Charlotte Q2 2017—Q1 2019

SINGLE FAMILY HOME SALES

QUARTER	Q2 2017	Q3 2017	Q4 2017	Q1 2018	Q2 2018	Q3 2018	Q4 2018	Q1 2019
# SOLD	689	611	542	588	689	589	503	508
YR/YR 5 QTR # CHANGE					0	-22	-39	-80
YR/YR 5 QTR % CHANGE					0.00%	-3.60%	-7.20%	-13.61%
$ MEDIAN SALE	176000	185000	174444	177725	193000	185000	192000	190000
4 QTR $ CHANGE				1725	8000	10556	14275	-3000
4 QTR % CHANGE				0.98%	4.32%	6.05%	8.03%	-1.55%
YR/YR 5 QTR $ CHANGE					17000	0	17556	12275
YR/YR 5 QTR % CHANGE					9.66%	0.00%	10.06%	6.91%
MID-RANGE SALES:								
$ LOWER 1/4	134500	139900	132000	140250	150000	145000	147500	152000
$ UPPER 1/4	243015	246000	238000	250950	261500	250000	251000	267500
$ HIGH SALE	1275000	1350000	1000000	1375000	1500000	1690500	1100000	916500

YR/QTR. ENDING: 1st 2017   2nd   3rd   4th   1st 2018   2nd   3rd   4th   1st 2019

PUNTA GORDA

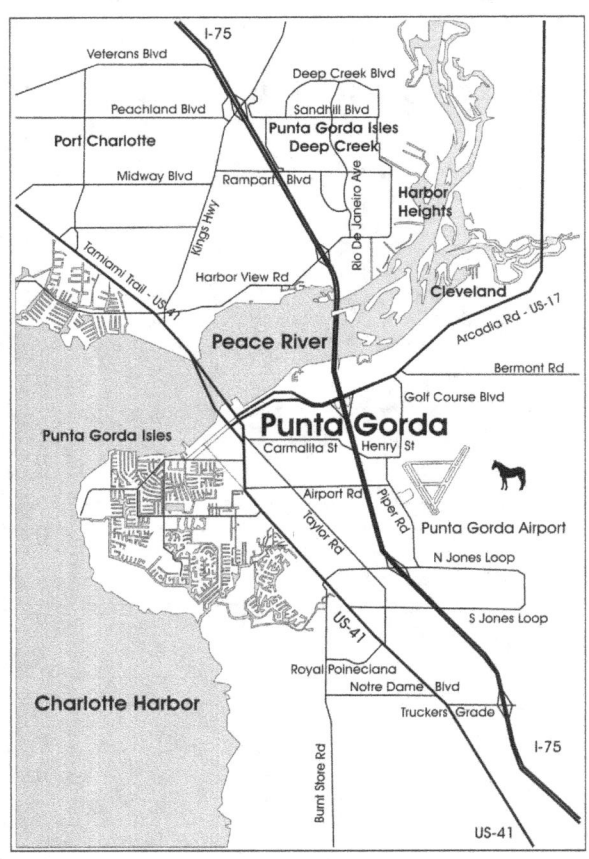

PUNTA GORDA

Single Family Home Sales

Q1 2019 Buying Power Chart

Market Segment - Median:	Price		Bed	Bath	Sq Ft Heated
Top Sale - maximum	$	945,000	6	6	4813
Upper 1/16	$	631,000	3	3	2541
Upper 1/8	$	540,000	3	3	2348
Upper 1/4	$	420,000	3	2	2215
Median	$	267,750	3	2	1894
Lower 1/4	$	214,000	3	2	1672
Lower1/8	$	179,500	3	2	1442
Lower 1/16	$	148,000	3	2	1248
Low Sale - minimum	$	64,000	1	1	744

Punta Gorda Q2 2017—Q1 2019

SINGLE FAMILY HOME SALES

QUARTER	Q2 2017	Q3 2017	Q4 2017	Q1 2018	Q2 2018	Q3 2018	Q4 2018	Q1 2019
# SOLD	370	292	302	308	392	263	293	282
YR/YR 5 QTR # CHANGE					22	-29	-9	-26
YR/YR 5 QTR % CHANGE					5.95%	-9.93%	-2.98%	-8.44%
$ MEDIAN SALE	240000	250000	260000	280000	280000	262000	272000	267750
4 QTR $ CHANGE				40000	30000	2000	-8000	-12250
4 QTR % CHANGE				16.67%	12.00%	0.77%	-2.86%	-4.38%
YR/YR 5 QTR $ CHANGE					40000	12000	12000	-12250
YR/YR 5 QTR % CHANGE					16.67%	4.80%	4.62%	-4.38%
MID-RANGE SALES:								
$ LOWER 1/4	190000	194350	204500	213000	219000	216765	219900	214000
$ UPPER 1/4	385000	375000	362500	430000	415000	417500	390000	420000
$ HIGH SALE	1150000	1775000	1023283	1150500	1560000	1295000	1200000	945000

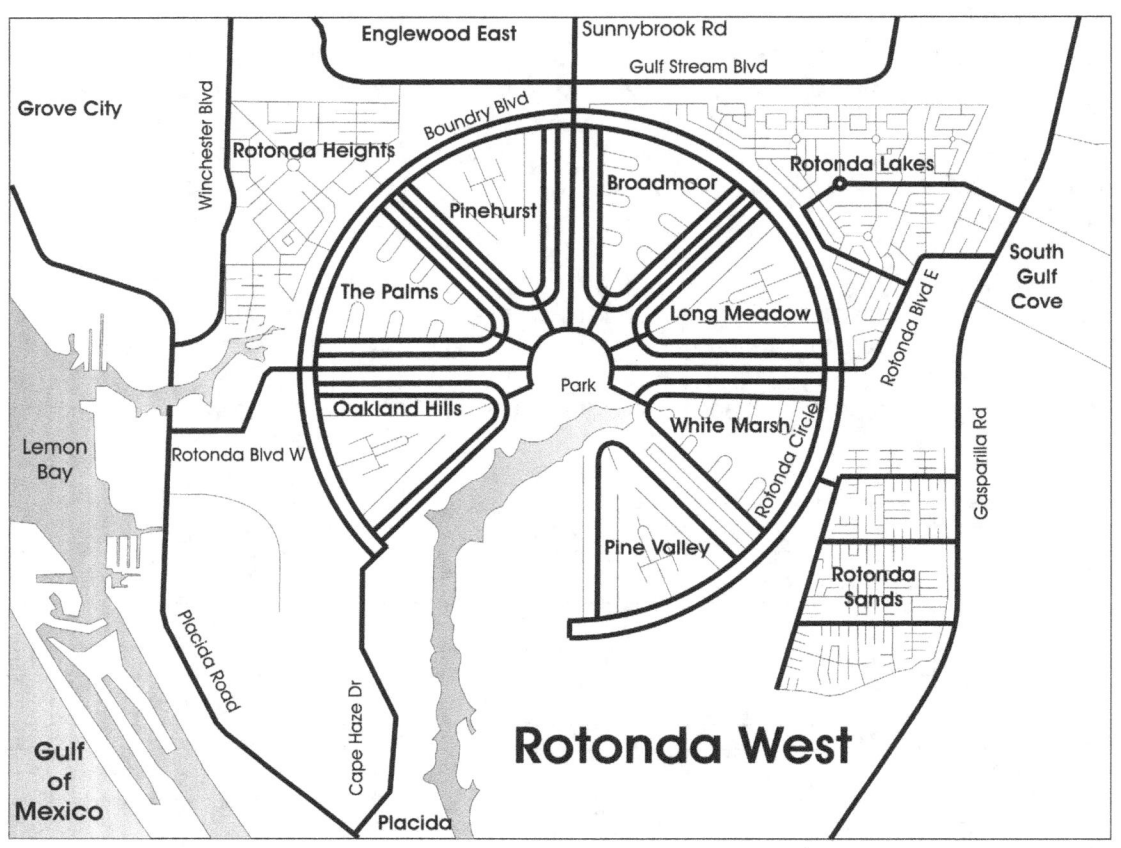

ROTONDA WEST

Single Family Home Sales

Q1 2019 Buying Power Chart

Market Segment - Median:	Price	Bed	Bath	Sq Ft Heated
Top Sale - maximum	$ 458,000	4	5	3062
Upper 1/16	$ 387,150	3	2	2107
Upper 1/8	$ 361,900	3	2	2092
Upper 1/4	$ 329,750	3	2	2069
Median	$ 270,000	3	2	1892
Lower 1/4	$ 212,500	3	2	1662
Lower1/8	$ 182,500	3	2	1524
Lower 1/16	$ 170,000	2	2	1524
Low Sale - minimum	$ 80,000	2	2	1172

Rotonda West Q2 2017—Q1 2019

SINGLE FAMILY HOME SALES

QUARTER	Q2 2017	Q3 2017	Q4 2017	Q1 2018	Q2 2018	Q3 2018	Q4 2018	Q1 2019
# SOLD	114	108	85	75	134	102	75	92
YR/YR 5 QTR # CHANGE					20	-6	-10	17
YR/YR 5 QTR % CHANGE					17.54%	-5.56%	-11.76%	22.67%
$ MEDIAN SALE	255500	260000	265000	242000	259000	244250	272000	270000
4 QTR $ CHANGE				-13500	-1000	-20750	30000	11000
4 QTR % CHANGE				-5.28%	-0.38%	-7.83%	12.40%	4.25%
YR/YR 5 QTR $ CHANGE					3500	-15750	7000	28000
YR/YR 5 QTR % CHANGE					1.37%	-6.06%	2.64%	11.57%
MID-RANGE SALES:								
$ LOWER 1/4	210000	222750	221750	207500	216500	212500	222500	212500
$ UPPER 1/4	289000	321000	305000	285000	311000	285000	335000	329750
$ HIGH SALE	400000	470000	485000	412500	492000	400000	498661	458000

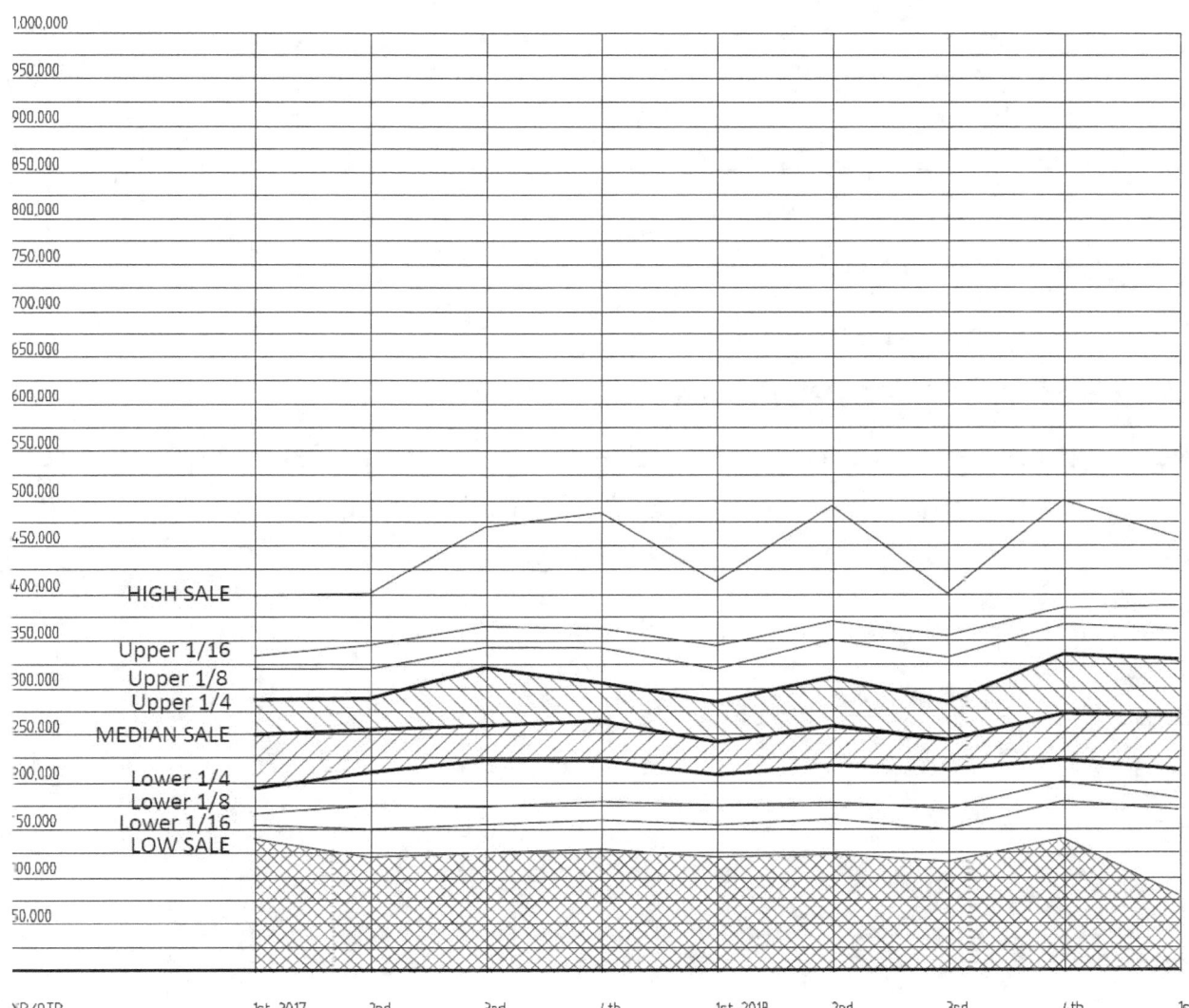

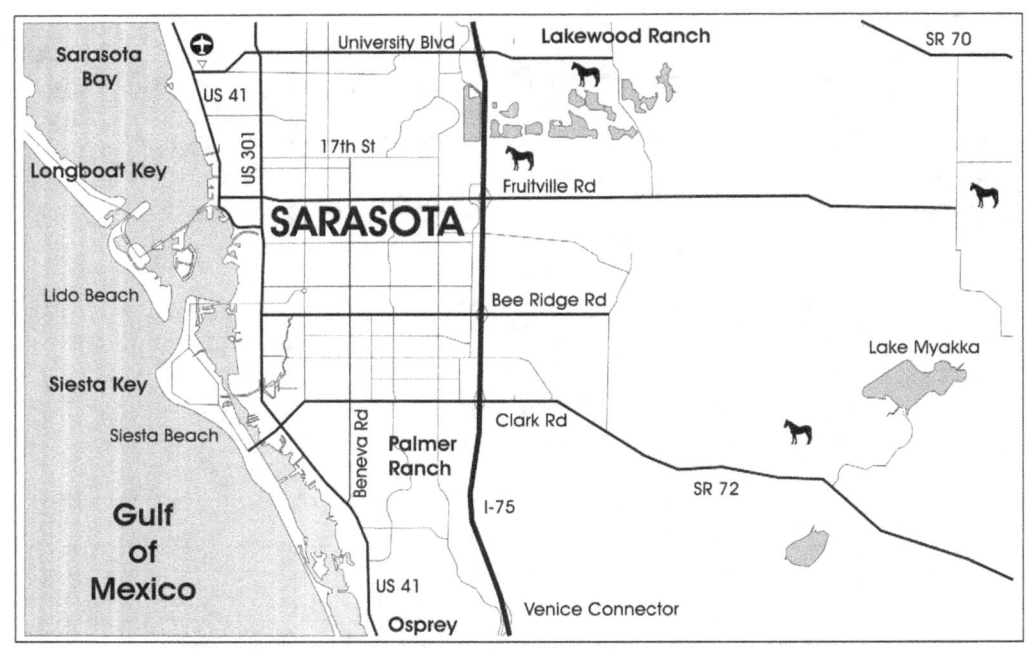

SARASOTA

Single Family Home Sales

Q1 2019 Buying Power Chart

Market Segment - Median:	Price	Bed	Bath	Sq Ft Heated
Top Sale - maximum	$ 9,850,000	6	7	7074
Upper 1/16	$ 1,012,500	4	4	3169
Upper 1/8	$ 702,736	4	3	2908
Upper 1/4	$ 476,350	3	3	2432
Median	$ 318,000	3	2	1830
Lower 1/4	$ 239,450	3	2	1439
Lower1/8	$ 202,000	3	2	1255
Lower 1/16	$ 175,000	2	2	1156
Low Sale - minimum	$ 27,000	1	1	644

Sarasota Q2 2017—Q1 2019

SINGLE FAMILY HOME SALES

QUARTER	Q2 2017	Q3 2017	Q4 2017	Q1 2018	Q2 2018	Q3 2018	Q4 2018	Q1 2019
# SOLD	**1120**	**939**	**873**	**882**	**1178**	**970**	**828**	**863**
YR/YR 5 QTR # CHANGE					58	31	-45	-19
YR/YR 5 QTR % CHANGE					5.18%	3.30%	-5.15%	-2.15%
$ MEDIAN SALE	**310000**	**310000**	**320000**	**314900**	**315000**	**313750**	**310000**	**318000**
4 QTR $ CHANGE				4900	5000	-6250	-4900	3000
4 QTR % CHANGE				1.58%	1.61%	-1.95%	-1.56%	0.95%
YR/YR 5 QTR $ CHANGE					5000	3750	-10000	3100
YR/YR 5 QTR % CHANGE					1.61%	1.21%	-3.13%	0.98%
MID-RANGE SALES:								
$ LOWER 1/4	227000	230000	235000	230000	238000	239000	237000	239450
$ UPPER 1/4	459979	445000	470000	475000	482500	442000	450000	476350
$ HIGH SALE	6350000	9000000	7453359	4800000	7000000	5675000	5850000	9850000
$ UPPER 1/16	874524	957500	1128100	1150000	1160000	897000	831000	1012500

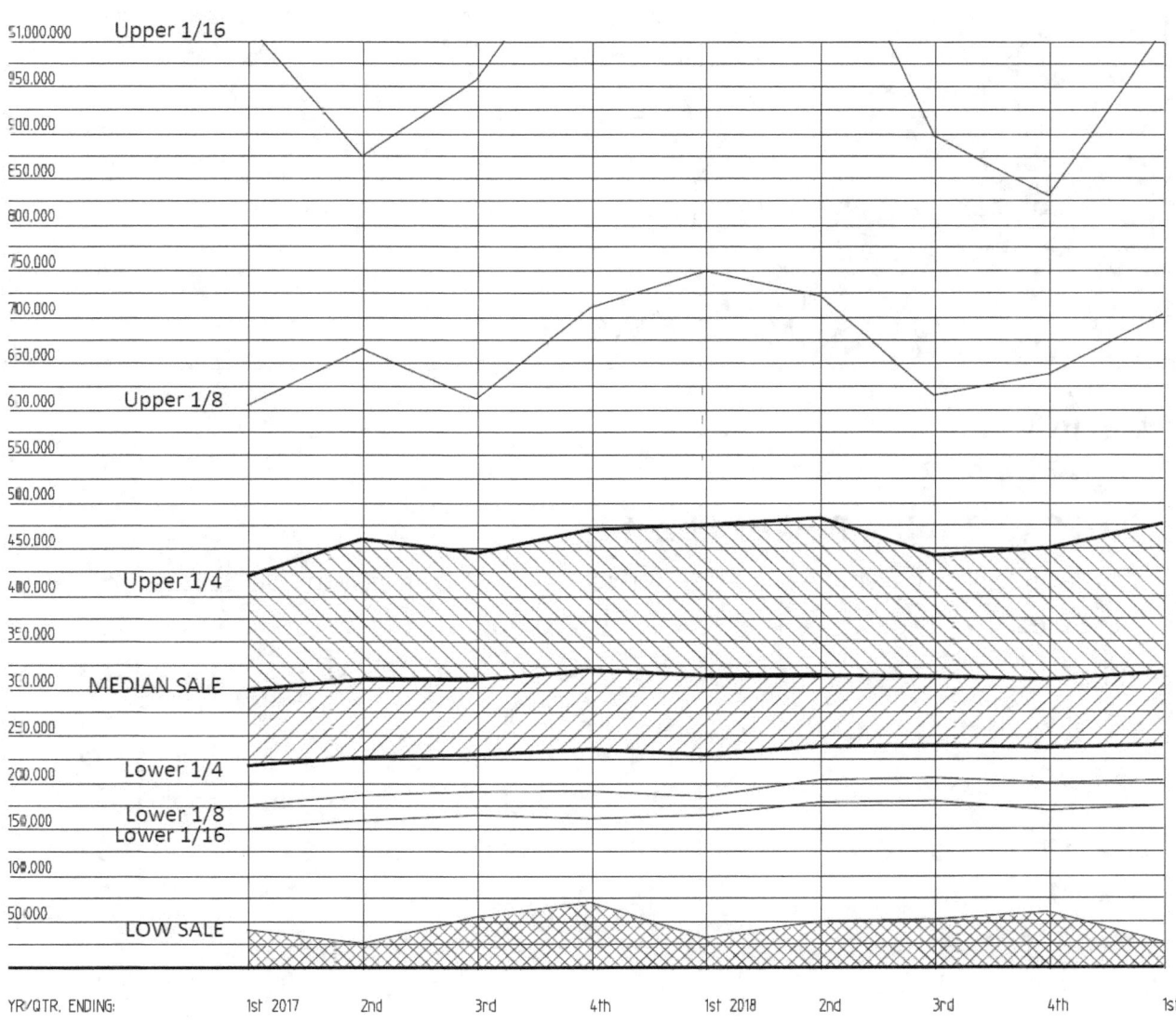

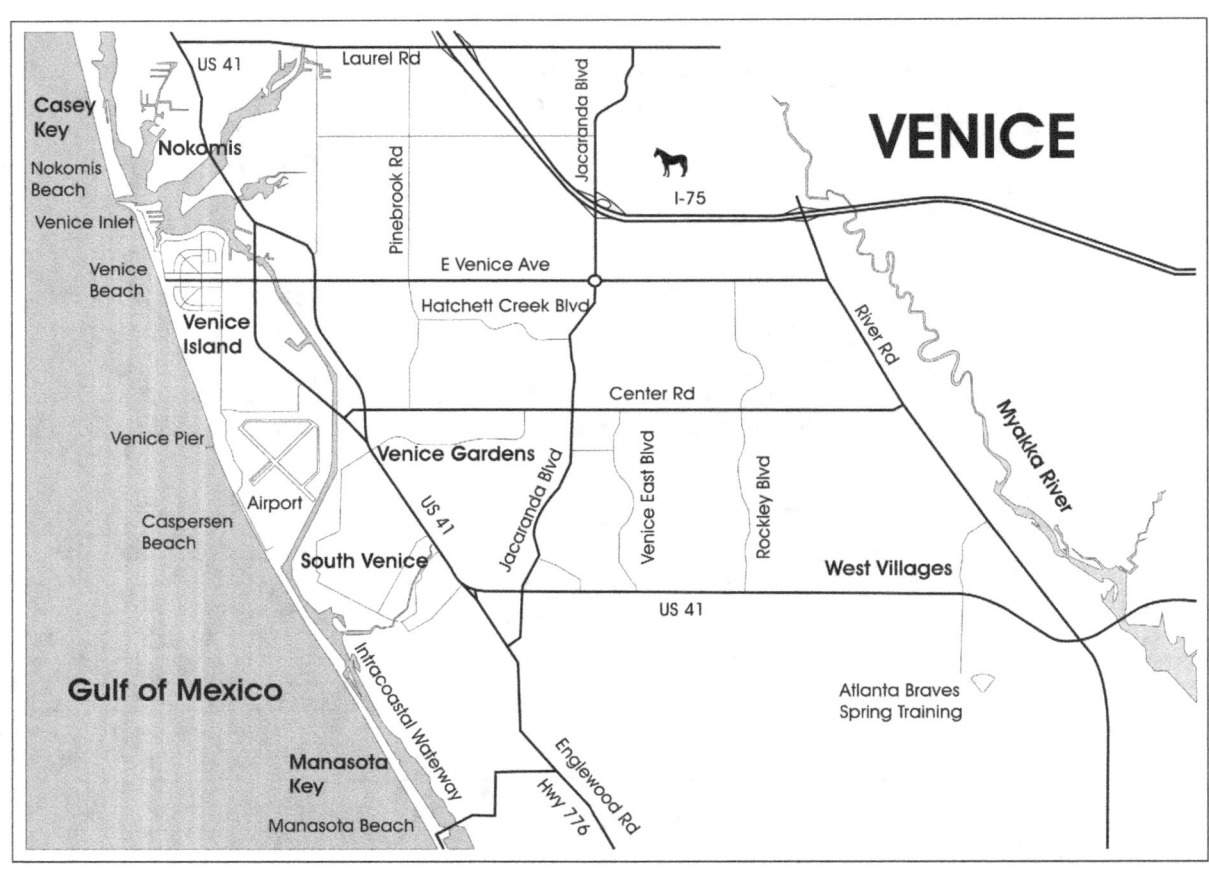

VENICE

Single Family Home Sales

Q1 2019 Buying Power Chart

Market Segment - Median:	Price	Bed	Bath	Sq Ft Heated
Top Sale - maximum	$ 1,500,000	6	5	4726
Upper 1/16	$ 537,000	3	3	2488
Upper 1/8	$ 445,000	3	3	2300
Upper 1/4	$ 375,000	3	2	2102
Median	$ 299,900	3	2	1816
Lower 1/4	$ 226,000	3	2	1508
Lower 1/8	$ 195,700	2	2	1280
Lower 1/16	$ 166,250	2	2	1190
Low Sale - minimum	$ 100,000	2	1	681

Venice Q2 2017— Q1 2019

SINGLE FAMILY HOME SALES

QUARTER	Q2 2017	Q3 2017	Q4 2017	Q1 2018	Q2 2018	Q3 2018	Q4 2018	Q1 2019
# SOLD	**528**	**419**	**412**	**379**	**563**	**419**	**394**	**391**
YR/YR 5 QTR # CHANGE					35	0	-18	12
YR/YR 5 QTR % CHANGE					6.63%	0.00%	-4.37%	3.17%
$ MEDIAN SALE	**291250**	**267500**	**295000**	**287000**	**295000**	**299000**	**299000**	**299900**
4 QTR $ CHANGE				-4250	27500	4000	12000	4900
4 QTR % CHANGE				-1.46%	10.28%	1.36%	4.18%	1.66%
YR/YR 5 QTR $ CHANGE					3750	31500	4000	12900
YR/YR 5 QTR % CHANGE					1.29%	11.78%	1.36%	4.49%
MID-RANGE SALES:								
$ LOWER 1/4	214950	208450	221500	215000	227000	232500	225000	226000
$ UPPER 1/4	370000	355000	365398	365000	372500	376750	372547	375000
$ HIGH SALE	2850000	1060000	2740000	2185000	8600000	2200000	2000000	1500000

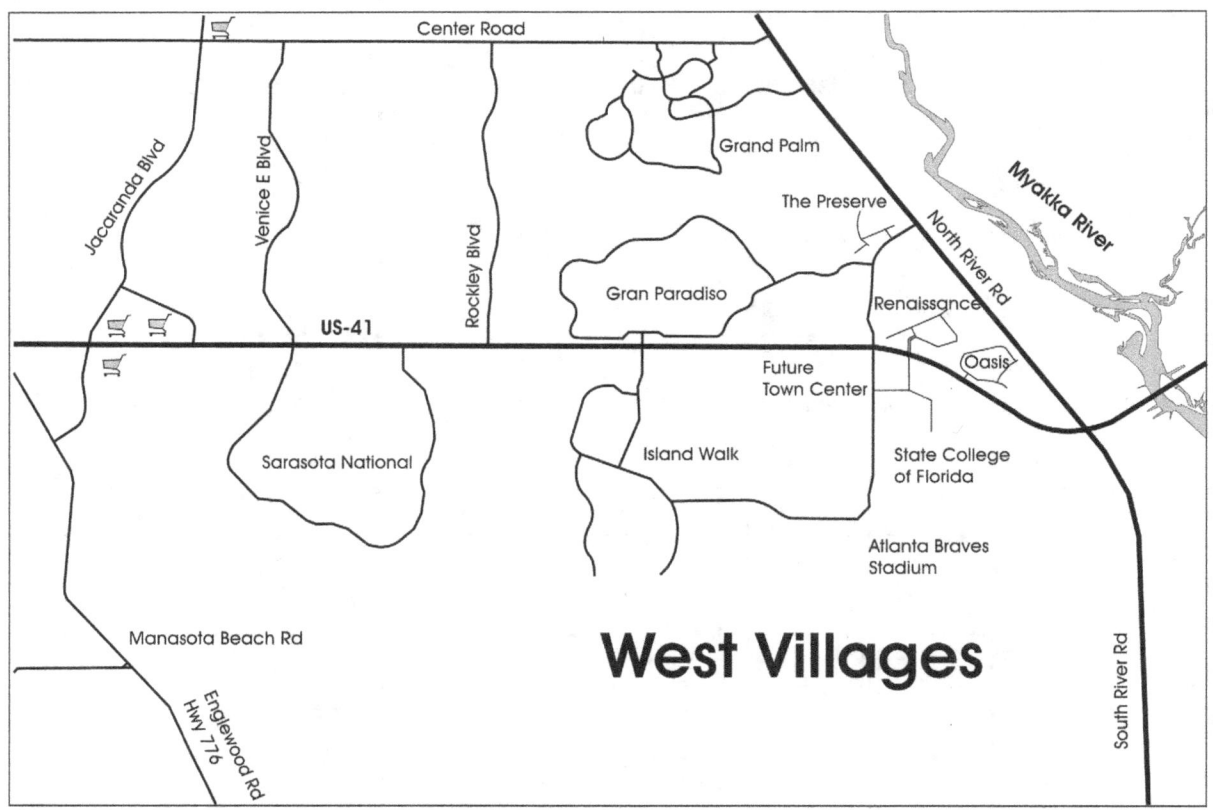

WEST VILLAGES

Single Family Home Sales

Q1 2019 Buying Power Chart

Market Segment - Median:	Price	Bed	Bath	Sq Ft Heated
Top Sale - maximum	$ 655,296	6	5	3867
Upper 1/16	$ 540,000	3	3	2749
Upper 1/8	$ 451,000	3	3	2488
Upper 1/4	$ 420,000	3	3	2239
Median	$ 355,496	3	2	2000
Lower 1/4	$ 308,496	3	2	1700
Lower1/8	$ 275,500	2	2	1576
Lower 1/16	$ 262,000	3	2	1437
Low Sale - minimum	$ 225,000	2	2	1080

West Villages Q2 2017— Q1 2019

SINGLE FAMILY HOME SALES

QUARTER	Q1 2017	Q2 2017	Q3 2017	Q4 2017	Q1 2018	Q2 2018	Q3 2018	Q1 2019
# SOLD	**40**	**63**	**58**	**90**	**53**	**110**	**87**	**85**
YR/YR 5 QTR # CHANGE					13	47	29	-5
YR/YR 5 QTR % CHANGE					32.50%	74.60%	50.00%	-5.56%
$ MEDIAN SALE	**327450**	**270000**	**360515**	**336400**	**352000**	**366287**	**347249**	**355496**
4 QTR $ CHANGE				8950	82000	5772	10849	3496
4 QTR % CHANGE				2.73%	30.37%	1.60%	3.23%	0.99%
YR/YR 5 QTR $ CHANGE					24550	96287	-13266	19096
YR/YR 5 QTR % CHANGE					7.50%	35.66%	-3.68%	5.68%
MID-RANGE SALES:								
$ LOWER 1/4	264364	334850	324744	290744	309900	304000	295000	308496
$ UPPER 1/4	386125	445898	450000	415000	399892	424000	434000	420000
$ HIGH SALE	603808	619800	679000	695000	778160	650000	682895	655296

ISLANDS, KEYS & MYAKKA CITY

Anna Maria, Bradenton Beach, Holmes Beach

Single Family Homes

Qtr/Year	Q2/2017	Q3/2017	Q4/2017	Q1/2018	Q2/2018	Q3/2018	Q4/2018	Q1/2019
Number Sold	81	51	43	59	72	54	38	48
$ High Sale	3525000	3351111	4500000	4500000	3000000	5000000	3300000	2550000
$ Median Sale	868000	1000000	865000	860000	842500	817500	875000	1050000
$ Low Sale	270000	385000	445000	290000	340000	265000	465000	380000

Condominiums

	Q2/2017	Q3/2017	Q4/2017	Q1/2018	Q2/2018	Q3/2018	Q4/2018	Q1/2019
Number Sold	35	33	32	24	48	32	22	19
$ High Sale	1650000	1700000	1225000	1120000	1999000	755000	1650000	950000
$ Median Sale	330000	385000	329500	422500	395000	338950	352500	357500
$ Low Sale	175000	233900	175000	230000	222500	202500	210000	180000

Longboat Key

Single Family Homes

Qtr/Year	Q2/2017	Q3/2017	Q4/2017	Q1/2018	Q2/2018	Q3/2018	Q4/2018	Q1/2019
Number Sold	31	25	26	37	38	25	17	21
$ High Sale	4100000	4500000	5825000	6800000	7000000	6880000	3000000	3825000
$ Median Sale	1270000	1050000	1028750	1072000	895000	915000	1200000	1260000
$ Low Sale	437000	290000	455000	496000	351000	435000	585000	275000

Condominiums

	Q2/2017	Q3/2017	Q4/2017	Q1/2018	Q2/2018	Q3/2018	Q4/2018	Q1/2019
Number Sold	113	80	55	98	137	80	47	87
$ High Sale	5500000	3200000	4800000	3100000	5500000	3000000	3275000	3362500
$ Median Sale	550000	481250	445000	585000	490000	482500	500000	550000
$ Low Sale	150000	187500	162500	190000	165000	160000	220000	166000

Lido, St Armands, and Bird Keys

Single Family Homes

Qtr/Year	Q2/2017	Q3/2017	Q4/2017	Q1/2018	Q2/2018	Q3/2018	Q4/2018	Q1/2019
Number Sold	19	13	17	21	30	10	5	14
$ High Sale	6350000	3250000	6180000	3965000	7000000	3150000	2925000	4450000
$ Median Sale	1675125	1800000	1250000	1420000	1617500	1649500	1825000	1265500
$ Low Sale	480000	695000	695000	500000	710000	825000	772500	415000

Condominiums

Number Sold	32	16	14	13	31	9	17	14
$ High Sale	4350000	4300000	4450000	3300000	5000000	1625000	3500000	2425000
$ Median Sale	439250	625000	563750	630000	462000	482500	382000	415000
$ Low Sale	175000	250000	250000	266800	197000	287500	229000	260000

Siesta Key

Single Family Homes

Qtr/Year	Q2/2017	Q3/2017	Q4/2017	Q1/2018	Q2/2018	Q3/2018	Q4/2018	Q1/2019
Number Sold	48	31	35	42	52	37	23	41
$ High Sale	4150000	9000000	7453359	3400000	3300000	5675000	5850000	6000000
$ Median Sale	833250	1106500	1100000	1089000	820000	830000	1000000	820000
$ Low Sale	400000	393500	471000	352275	385000	412125	470000	325000

Condominiums

Number Sold	87	64	59	82	93	81	39	60
$ High Sale	2200000	2250000	1160000	2600000	3500000	2630000	879400	2400000
$ Median Sale	509000	485000	460000	485000	525000	489000	468000	480000
$ Low Sale	64000	229000	247500	90000	65000	75000	220000	68000

Casey Key

Single Family Homes

Qtr/Year	Q2/2017	Q3/2017	Q4/2017	Q1/2018	Q2/2018	Q3/2018	Q4/2018	Q1/2019
Number Sold	2	6	1	4	4	3	3	5
$ High Sale	1600000	6550000	1825000	3075000	4500000	4000000	6100000	5300000
$ Median Sale	1150000	1500000	1825000	1700000	2875000	830000	3550000	3630000
$ Low Sale	700000	1200000	1825000	950000	1600000	549000	1900000	1200000

Condominiums

	Q2/2017	Q3/2017	Q4/2017	Q1/2018	Q2/2018	Q3/2018	Q4/2018	Q1/2019
Number Sold	1	0	1	1	0	0	0	0
$ High Sale	435000		290000	485000				
$ Median Sale	435000		290000	485000				
$ Low Sale	435000		290000	485000				

Manasota Key

Single Family Homes

Qtr/Year	Q2/2017	Q3/2017	Q4/2017	Q1/2018	Q2/2018	Q3/2018	Q4/2018	Q1/2019
Number Sold	10	8	3	5	15	7	6	8
$ High Sale	3500000	3250000	1200000	2300000	4650000	3000000	1700000	3050000
$ Median Sale	515000	1350000	680000	1675000	776000	844000	642225	915000
$ Low Sale	310000	300000	546000	382000	265000	400000	396000	331000

Condominiums

	Q2/2017	Q3/2017	Q4/2017	Q1/2018	Q2/2018	Q3/2018	Q4/2018	Q1/2019
Number Sold	20	14	4	16	38	15	18	19
$ High Sale	1500000	1330000	505000	762000	940000	1350000	450000	949500
$ Median Sale	378000	302000	387500	365000	293750	310500	252500	239900
$ Low Sale	122000	185000	255000	229900	162000	219900	159000	117500

Placida - Palm Island, Little Gasparilla Island, Don Pedro Island
Single Family Homes

Qtr/Year	Q2/2017	Q3/2017	Q4/2017	Q1/2018	Q2/2018	Q3/2018	Q4/2018	Q1/2019
Number Sold	34	24	21	23	19	19	17	21
$ High Sale	1525000	1100000	2375000	919900	1025000	2125000	846000	1050000
$ Median Sale	483750	388801	420000	348000	406500	530000	370100	515000
$ Low Sale	184900	189500	220000	170000	249000	209000	225500	243000

Condominiums

Qtr/Year	Q2/2017	Q3/2017	Q4/2017	Q1/2018	Q2/2018	Q3/2018	Q4/2018	Q1/2019
Number Sold	26	5	23	13	28	11	9	11
$ High Sale	865000	870000	450000	1050000	850000	630000	710000	615000
$ Median Sale	276000	349900	254000	255000	276250	280000	265000	245000
$ Low Sale	130000	160000	145000	125000	155000	140000	150000	150000

Myakka City - Manatee County - Rural & Acreage Properties
Single Family Homes

Qtr/Year	Q2/2017	Q3/2017	Q4/2017	Q1/2018	Q2/2018	Q3/2018	Q4/2018	Q1/2019
Number Sold	14	20	26	23	19	16	14	11
$ High Sale	670000	1330000	1100000	500000	2350000	670000	1225000	650000
$ Median Sale	395000	352450	352500	295000	340000	364950	359750	415000
$ Low Sale	162500	230000	244829	184900	190000	175000	195000	215000